Street by Street

TRURO
FALMOUTH
PENRYN, ST MAWES

Devoran, Feock, Flushing, Gerrans, Mylor Bridge, Probus, St Just in Roseland, Trelissick, Tresillian, Trewithian

1st edition May 2001

© Automobile Association Developments Limited 2001

This product includes map data licensed from Ordnance Survey® with the permission of the Controller of Her Majesty's Stationery Office. © Crown copyright 2000. All rights reserved. Licence No: 399221.

Published by AA Publishing (a trading name of Automobile Association Developments Limited, whose registered office is Norfolk House, Priestley Road, Basingstoke, Hampshire, RG24 9NY. Registered number 1878835).

Mapping produced by the Cartographic Department of The Automobile Association.

A CIP Catalogue record for this book is available from the British Library.

Printed by GRAFIASA S.A., Porto, Portugal

The contents of this atlas are believed to be correct at the time of the latest revision. However, the publishers cannot be held responsible for loss occasioned to any person acting or refraining from action as a result of any material in this atlas, nor for any errors, omissions or changes in such material. The publishers would welcome information to correct any errors or omissions and to keep this atlas up to date. Please write to Publishing, The Automobile Association, Fanum House, Basing View, Basingstoke, Hampshire, RG21 4EA.

Ref: ML115

Key to map pages ii-iii

Key to map symbols iv-1

Enlarged scale pages 2-5

Street by Street 6-57

Index – towns & villages 58

Index – streets 59-

Index – featured places

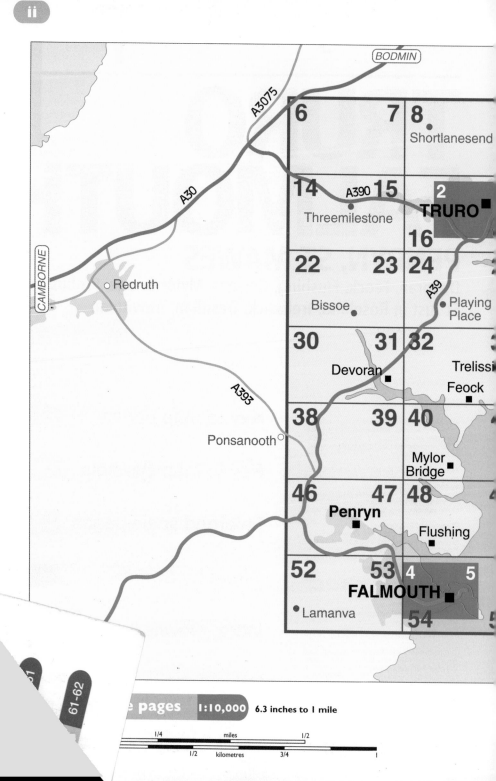

BODMIN

A3075

A30

CAMBORNE

| 6 | 7 | 8 |
Shortlanesend

| 14 | A390 15 | 2 TRURO |
Threemilestone
16

| 22 | 23 | 24 |
Bissoe
A39
Playing Place

| 30 | 31 | 32 |
Devoran
Trelissi
Feock

| 38 | 39 | 40 |
A393
Ponsanooth
Mylor Bridge

| 46 | 47 | 48 |
Penryn
Flushing

| 52 | 53 | 4 | 5 |
FALMOUTH
Lamanva
54

Redruth

61-62

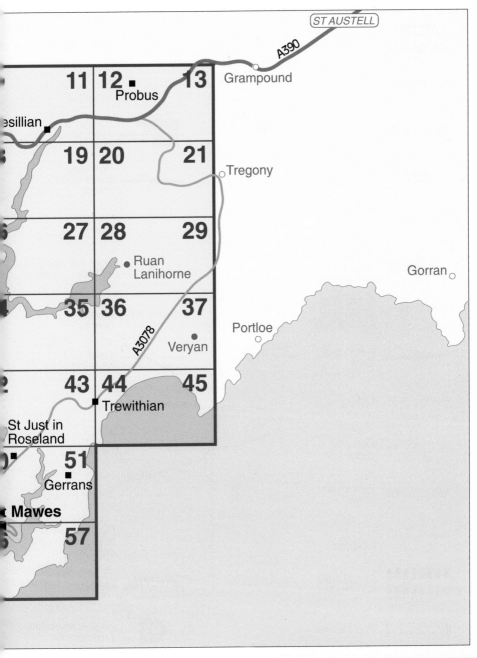

ST AUSTELL

A390

11 | 12 ▪ | 13   Grampound
    Probus

esillian ▪

19 | 20 | 21   Tregony

27 | 28 | 29   Gorran ○

Ruan
Lanihorne ●

35 | 36 | 37   Portloe ○

A3078

Veryan ●

43 | 44 | 45
  ▪ Trewithian

St Just in
Roseland

▪

51
  ▪
Gerrans

Mawes

57

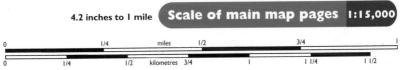

4.2 inches to 1 mile   **Scale of main map pages** 1:15,000

0   1/4   miles   1/2   3/4   1
0   1/4   1/2   kilometres 3/4   1   1 1/4   1 1/2

Junction 9	Motorway & junction	P+🚌	Park & Ride
Services	Motorway service area	🚌	Bus/Coach station
	Primary road single/dual carriageway		Railway & main railway station
Services	Primary road service area		Railway & minor railway station
	A road single/dual carriageway	⊖	Underground station
	B road single/dual carriageway	⊖	Light Railway & station
	Other road single/dual carriageway	+++++++++	Preserved private railway
	Restricted road	LC	Level crossing
	Private road	•—•—•—•	Tramway
← ←	One way street	----------	Ferry route
	Pedestrian street	....	Airport runway
-----------	Track/ footpath	– · – · – · –	Boundaries- borough/ district
	Road under construction	＼＼＼＼＼＼	Mounds
[– – –]	Road tunnel	93	Page continuation 1:15,000
P	Parking	7	Page continuation to enlarged scale 1:10,000

	River/canal, lake, pier	🚻	Toilet with disabled facilities
	Aqueduct, lock, weir	🅿	Petrol station
465 ▲ Winter Hill	Peak (with height in metres)	PH	Public house
	Beach	PO	Post Office
	Coniferous woodland	📖	Public library
	Broadleaved woodland	𝒊	Tourist Information Centre
	Mixed woodland	♖	Castle
	Park	🏛	Historic house/ building
	Cemetery	Wakehurst Place NT	National Trust property
	Built-up area	🏛 M	Museum/ art gallery
	Featured building	†	Church/chapel
⊓⊔⊓⊔⊓⊔	City wall	♆	Country park
A&E	Accident & Emergency hospital	🎭	Theatre/ performing arts
🚻	Toilet	🎥	Cinema

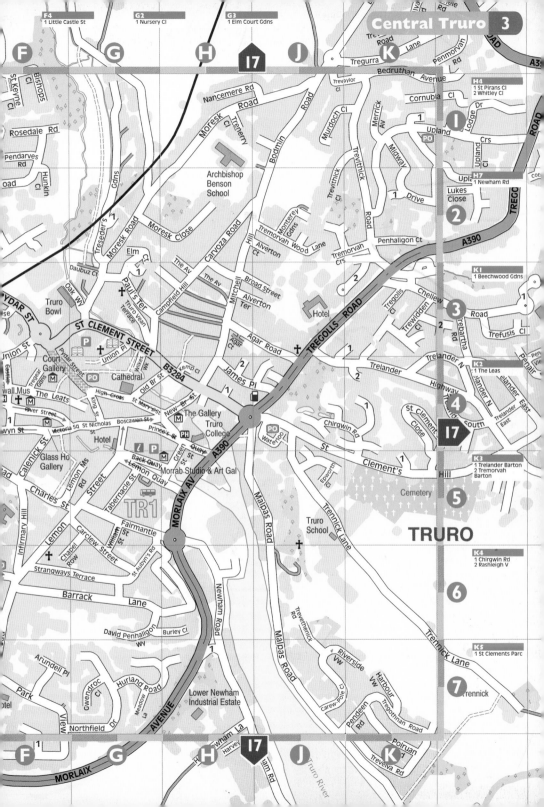

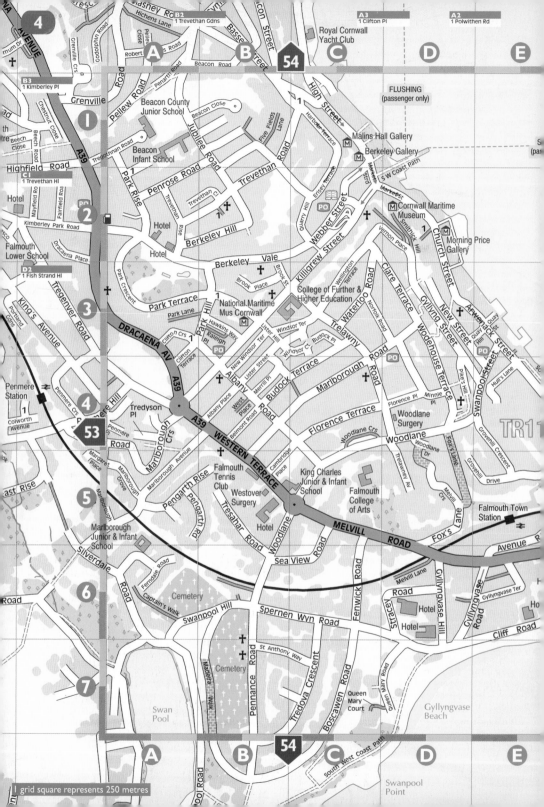

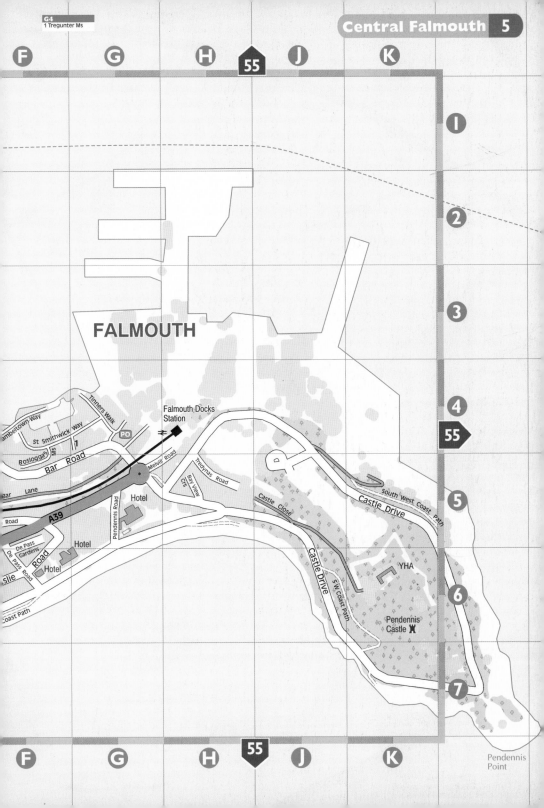

G4
1 Tregunter Ms

F G H **55** J K

I

2

3

4

55

5

6

7

FALMOUTH

Tinners Walk

Ambertown Way

St Smithwick Way

Bosloggas

Bar Road

PO

Bar Lane

A39

Pendennis Road

Road

De Pass Gardens

De Pass Road

Hotel

Hotel

Hotel

Leslie Road

Coast Path

Melvill Road

Falmouth Docks
Station

Bay View Crs

Tredynas Road

Castle Close

Castle Drive

S W Coast Path

South West Coast Path

Castle Drive

YHA

Pendennis Castle

F G H **55** J K

Pendennis
Point

Pendale

BS284

A3075

A30(T)

A

B

C

D

1

Garvinack

2

Causilgey

3

Silver
Valley

Trevaskis

Little
Croft West

4

Penstraze
Business
Centre

5

A390

A

B

14

C

D

Cro

West
Langarth

1 grid square represents 500 metres

B3284

Allet

E

Chybucca

F

Choon

G

H

I

Shortlane

2

Nancewrath

Roseworthy

3

Tregavethan
Manor

8

4

Treworder

5

River Kenwyn

E

F

15

G

H

Langarth

Governs

Penventinnie Lane

8

Ⓐ   Ⓑ   Ⓒ   Ⓓ

Garra

Trevellan

River Allen

I

B3284

CHURCH ROAD

Forge Way

Idless Lane

Ashley Rd

PO

2

Shortlanesend

Eglos Road

Northey Cl

Shortlanesend School

Hillcrest

Bosvean Road

School Hill

Carvinack

Bussavean

3

7

Treheveras

4

B3284

Featherbed

5

KENWYN ROAD

B3284

Boscolla

Ⓐ   Ⓑ   16   Ⓒ   **Denw**

Lane

KENWYN HILL

New Mill

Pencarrick Close

Kenwyn Cl

Kenwyn Church Rd

Knights Hl

1 grid square represents 500 metres

E   F   G   H

1

2

3

10

4

5

St Clement Woods

A39

Calerick

Penmount

Idless

Crematorium

Polwele House School

Killagorden

Buckshead

Tregurra

Nancemere

A39

17

E   F   G   H

Boumin Road

Treverbyn Rd

Pensliva Rd

Tregurra Lane

Penmorah Rd

NEWQUAY ROAD

UNION

1

Spires

Bishops Close

St Keyne

Chainwall Dr

2

Nancemere Rd

Bedruthan Avenue

Cornubia Cl

Lodge Dr

E2
1 Ashleigh Wy
2 Church View Rd

Tregoose

A390

E

F

G

H

I

Trenithan
Chancellor

Rosparc

Carne View Road

gery

Parkengear vean

arkengear

A390

Road

Trestrayle

2

3

4

5

A3078

E

F

21

G

H

ewater

Trewithen

14

a Pen
Business
Centre

A390

A B **6** C D

West
Langarth

Cre

1

Saveock

**Green
Bottom**

A390

Tre
VW

2

Lov
W

Threemilestone

5 Holly
C
Glenthorne R

3

Lead Pk

2

Lower Hugu

SPY

Tomperrow

4

Hugus

†

5

Kerley
Downs

†

A B **22** C D

1 grid square represents 500 metres

E3
1 Berveth Cl
2 Carlyon Cl
3 Linley Cl
4 Rosevalley
5 Sampson Wy

F3
1 Polstain Crs

E **F** **7** **G** **H**

River Kenwyn

Langarth

Governs

I

Penventinnie Lane

The Duchy Hospital

G3
1 Chyvelah Ope
2 Meadow Cl

Wren Industrial Estate

Oak   Lane

Treliske Hospital
A&E

Penventinnie Lane

2

H3
1 Nansavallon Rd

e

Royal Cornwall Hospital

Truro Golf Club

A390 TRESAWLS ROAD

TRESAWLS ROAD

Pendeen Crs
Victoria Gardens
Pendeen
Glyn Way
Pendeen Close
Polstain

Mount Pleasant Road

Road

Chyvelah Vale

Truro College

Gloweth

Gloweth View
Tresawls Av
Lamellyn Drive
Cryon Vw

3

Tre
Pe

Victoria Rd

3
5
2
1
1

4

Threemilestone County Primary School

1

Kingsley Cl

1
2

1

16

Newbridge Lane

Valley View
Dr
Vall View

Besore

Newbridge Lane

Evea Cl
Carrine Road

Hi

4

Newbridge

Penweat

Hugus Farm

5

E **F** **23** **G** **H**

Carrine Common

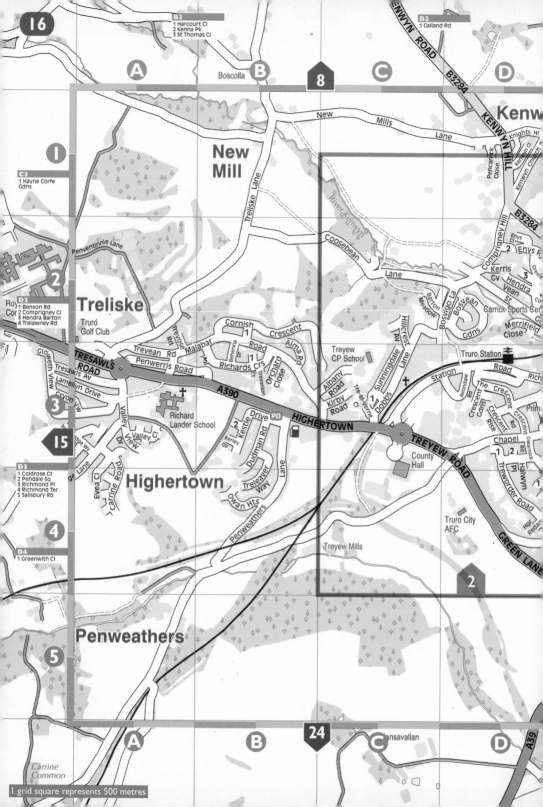

A **B** **8** **C** **D**

KENWYN ROAD B3284

Kenw

Boscolla

New   Mills   Lane

KENYON HILL

Knights Hl

New
Mill

Kenwyn Cl

Kenwyn Church

I

Pencarrick Close

C3
1 Hayne Corfe
Gdns

Treliske Lane

River Kenwyn

Comprigney Hill

Penventinnie Lane

Coosebean

Enys V

2
1 Enys R

Kerris
Gv

Hendra
Vean

2

Treliske

Lane

Barton

Bosvean

Bosvigo La

3

St

Ro
D2
1 Benson Rd
2 Comprigney Cl
3 Hendra Barton
4 Trelawney Rd
Cor

Truro
Golf Club

Meadow

Bosvigo
Gdns

Carrick Sports Cen

Merrifield
Close

Gl

Cornish

Crescent

Treyew
CP School

Truro Station

Hillcrest

1

Trevean Rd

Malabar

1

Richards Crs

Alma Rd

Av

Sunningdale

Station

Road

Rich

3

TRESAWLS
ROAD

Trevean Rd

Penwerris   Road

Behenna
Dr

Orchard
Close

Dobbs

The
Crescent

Rd

Gloweth View

Tresawis Av

Lamellyn Drive

A390

Trevanion

Albany
Road

Treverbyn

Avondale

Crescent
Gdns

Crescent
Rise

Prim

Tresawls Av

15

Cryon Vw

Richard
Lander School

2

Kestle

Drive

Kirby
Road

HIGHERTOWN

Chapel

Gwarnick
Rd

D3
1 Coldrose Ct
2 Pendale Sq
3 Richmond Pl
4 Richmond Ter
5 Salisbury Rd

Valley
View

Kerley
Gv

Dudman Rd

Lane

County
Hall

TREYEW   ROAD

1 **2**

Halwyn
Pl

Treworder Road

4

Eva Cl

Carrine Road

Highertown

Treleaver

Way

Owan Hts

D4
1 Greenwith Cl

Penweathers

Truro City
AFC

Hgr
Redan

GREEN LANE

2

Penweathers

Treyew Mills

5

A **B** **24** **C** ansavallan **D** A39

Carrine
Common

1 grid square represents 500 metres

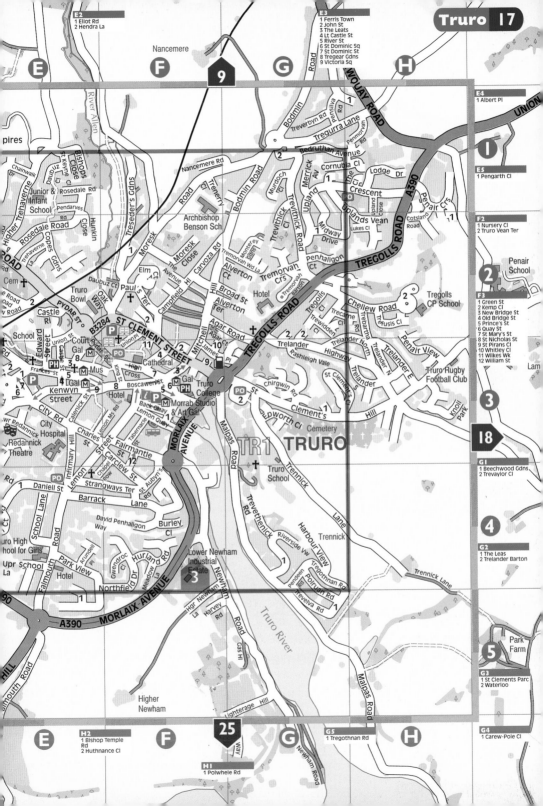

18

A   UNION   B   **10**   C   HILL   D

Polsue Manor
Farm

A390

1

Dr

A390

Penair Crs

17

Cotsland
Road

Penair

Penair View

2

Tregolls
CP School

Penair
School

Pencalenick
School

Pencalenic

2

Cl

andere E

Lambesso

Truro Rugby
Football Club

Tresillian River

3

Kiver
Park

17

Menadews
Farm

4

Trennick Lane

5

Park
Farm

†

St Clement

A   B   **26**   C   D

1 grid square represents 500 metres

Higher Polsue W...
Carne
Mdw
Polsue Way
Heron Close
PO
A390

E

F

G

H

Creekside View

Treffry

Carharthen

I

2

Tregerrick

3

20

Merther

4

Treveor

5

Tresawsan

E

F

27

G

H

Namprathic

Tregenna

Ga

Fentongollan

E **A3078** F **13** G H

I

ewater

Grogarth Farm

†

2

Killiow Farm

Tregony

3 Frog Lane
   TREGONY
   We
   Lar
   A3078

A3078

4

River Fal

Trelasker

5

Trewarthenick

E F **29** G H

Trethewey Farm

Kerley
Downs

A

B

14

C

D

I

2

3

Cusveorth
Coombe

Cross Lanes

Baldhu

Twelveheads

Tailings
Dam

Wheal B

4

5

Fernsplatt

Race

Hill

Coombe Lane

PO

Bissoe

Carnon River

Cem

A

B

30

C

D

Hick's Mill

Coldwind Cross

Coombe La

Cusgarne

Coombe

Hugus Farm

E   F   **15**   G   H

Carrine
Common

1

Goodern
Manor Farm

Pound   Lane

2

3

Sparnock
Farm

24

4

Helston
Water

Chyreen   Lane

5

Quenchwell

Quenchwell   Road

E   F   **31**   G   H

Grenna Lane

Valley   Lane
3   1   4
Forth   Nowth   Quen

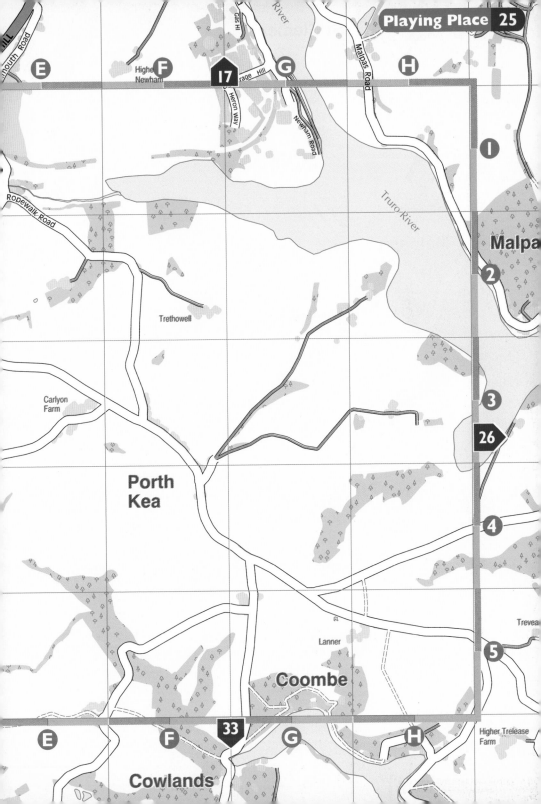

E

F

Higher
Newham

17

G

Malpas Road

H

River

Cas Hi

rage Hill

Heron Way

Newham Road

I

Truro River

Malpa

2

Ropewalk Road

Trethowell

3

26

Carlyon
Farm

**Porth
Kea**

4

Lanner

Trevea

5

Coombe

E

F

33

G

H

Higher Trelease
Farm

Cowlands

Park
Farm

St Clement

Ⓐ   Ⓑ   **18**   Ⓒ   Ⓓ

①

Tresillian River

River

Malpas

Malpas Road

②

PO

(passenger only)

Truro River

Tregonian

③

St
Pe

†

PO

Woodbury

**Old
Kea**

④

Tregot

⑤

Trevean

Higher Treleas
Farm

Ⓐ   Ⓑ   **34**   Ⓒ   Ⓓ

1 grid square represents 500 metres

E
F
19
G
H

Namprathic

Tregenna

I

Ga

Fentongollan

Merther Lane

2

Trewonnal

Lam
Woo

3

28

ael
vil

Lamorran

4

Nancarrow

5

River Fal

Penkevel

Ardevora
Veor

E
F
35
G
H

E   F   **21**   G   H

I

TR2

Trethewey Farm

Cregoe

2

Demain Farm

Penhesken

3

Tregongon

4

Treswithian   A3078

5

Tregisswyn

E   F   **37**   G   H   Ca

30

Fernsplatt

Bissoe

Carnon River

Race

Coombe Lane

Coombe La

A

B

C

D

✝

22

I

Cusgarne
School

Coombe

Hick's Mill

Coldwind Cross

Cusgarne

Pencantol

2

PO

Treneglos

ogpool

**Greenwith
Common**

Cemetery

Silver Hill

3

Greenwith

Road

Greenwith Road

Station Road

Hill

Perranwell

4

Westmoor
Crs

PO

Arworthal
Mdw

School

West Pk

Hill

St Piran's Hill

5

Treworthal
Road

Church Road

Trewinnard
Road

Upper
Tredrea

Cove Hill

Tredrea Gdns

Pellynwartha

Perranarworthal

M

The
Old Barn Gallery

A

B

38

Goonrea

C

A39

D

1 grid square represents 500 metres

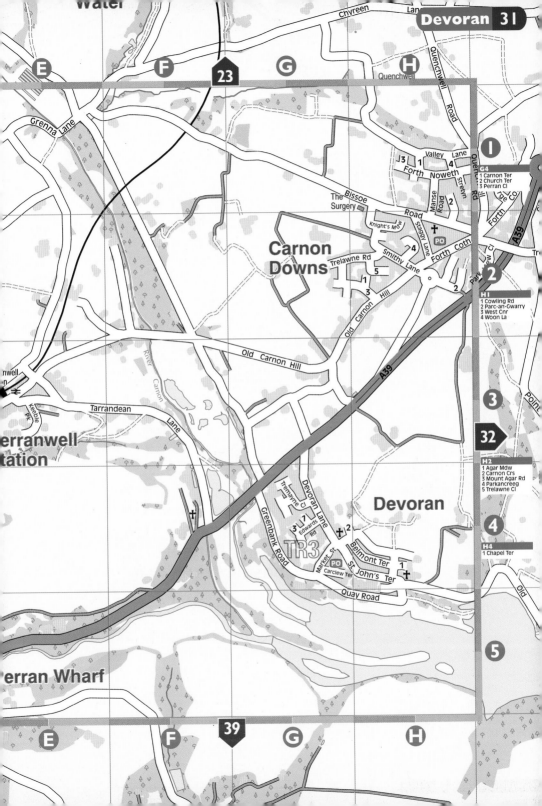

Water

Chyreen Lane

Quenchwell Road

Quenchwell

Grenna Lane

I

G4
1 Carnon Ter
2 Church Ter
3 Perran Cl

Valley Lane
3 1 4
Forth Noweth
Stretyn
The Bissoe Surgery
Manse Road

Knight's Mdw
Staggy Lane
Road
PO

Carnon Downs

Trelawne Rd
Smithy Lane
4
5
Forth Coth

1
3
Old Carnon Hill
2

2

H1
1 Cowling Rd
2 Parc-an-Gwarry
3 West Cnr
4 Woon La

Park

A39

Old Carnon Hill

A39

3

Point

River Carnon

Tarrandean
Lane

Keeble PK

32

erranwell tation

H2
1 Agar Mdw
2 Carnon Crs
3 Mount Agar Rd
4 Parkancreeg
5 Trelawne Cl

4

H4
1 Chapel Ter

Trenawne
Devoran Lane
7
Edwards Rd
3 1
Greenbank Road

Devoran

TR3

Market St
Carclew Ter
PO
St John's Ter
Belmont Ter
2
1

Quay Road

5

erran Wharf

Old

E F G H

39

E F G H

E5
1 Dozmere Cl
2 Gwel-an-Scol

Lanner

E

F

25

Coombe

G

H

Higher Trelease
Farm

I

Cowlands

ey

Tregew

2

B3289

Dicky Lane

3

34

Trelissick
Garden (NT)

KING HARRY
FERRY V

onpiper

Higher Trevilla

Trelissick

4

**Lower
Trevilla**

Pill Farm

5

Elm
Dr
Elm Gv

PO
gue

E

41

F

G

H

Tremayne
Ct

Feock

Green
Close

Turnaware
Point

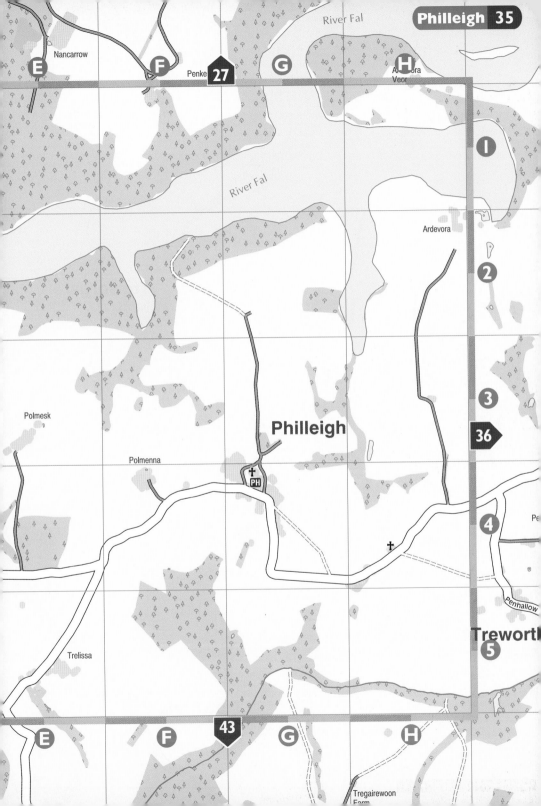

River Fal

E Nancarrow F Penke **27** G H Are ora Veor

I

River Fal

Ardevora

2

Polmesk

3

Philleigh

36

Polmenna

† PH

†

4

Pe

Penhallow

Treworth

Trelissa

5

E F **43** G H

Tregairewoon Farm

36

Ardevora
Veor

A

B

28

Trelonk

C

D

I

Tuckingmill Creek

Treviles

Ardevora

2

Treworga

Trenestrall

3

35

Polsue
Manor Hotel

Penhallow

4

Penhallow Close

Treworthal

5

Treworlas

A

B

44

C

D

Treluggan

1 grid square represents 500 metres

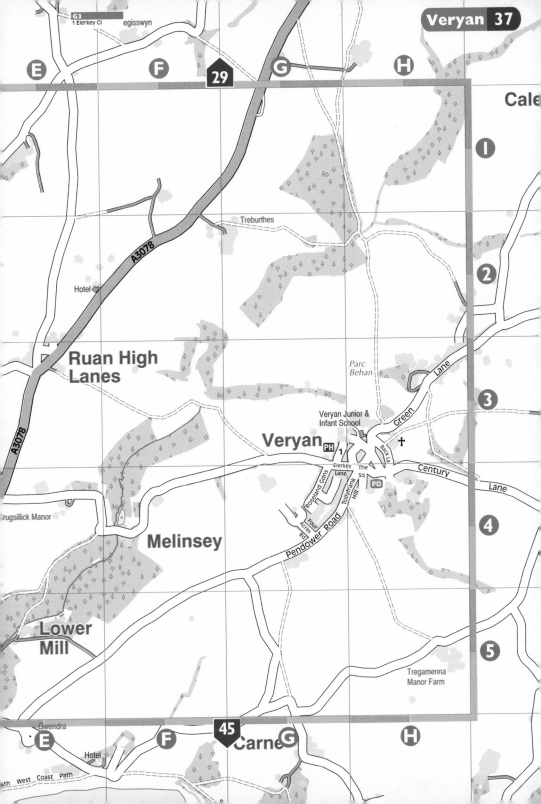

G3
1 Elerkey Cl   egisswyn

E   F   29   G   H

Cale

I

Treburthes

A3078

Hotel

2

Ruan High
Lanes

Parc
Behan

Veryan Junior &
Infant School

Green Lane

3

A3078

Veryan   PH 1

Elerkey
Lane

The
Sq

✝

Crugsillick Manor

Roseland Gdns

Tollyfrank Hill

PO

Century

Lane

4

Melinsey

Four
Acres
Rd

Pendower Road

Lower
Mill

Tregamenna
Manor Farm

5

Gwendra

E   F   45   Carne   G   H

Hotel

uth West Coast Path

erran Wharf

E F **31** G H

I

Carclew

2

Carclew Road

Angarrick

3

Stockdale

40

Mylor ridge

4

Broads

Lane

The Cogos

Park Close

Comfort Road

Willow Close

5

Enys

E F **47** G H

Gwarder

Carvinack

Woodlands

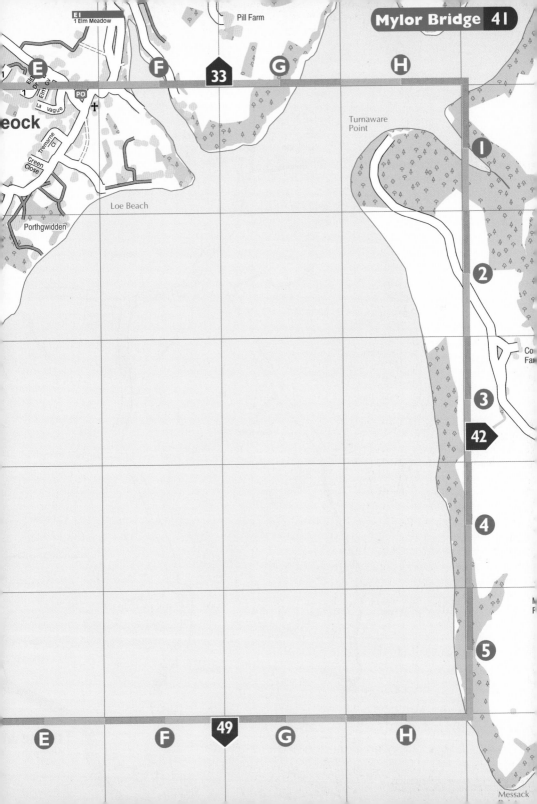

E1
1 Elm Meadow

Pill Farm

eock

PO

La Vague

Tremayne Ct

Green Close

Loe Beach

Porthgwidden

Turnaware
Point

Co
Fa

Messack

42

A   B   **34**   C   D

Penperth

1

Tolcarne

Treverras

2

Roscassa

Tredellans

Commerrans Farm

3

41

Carwarthen

4

Trethem

Messack Farm

Pulpry

Polhendra

5

Tregorland

B3289

A3078 MILL HI

A   B   **50**   C   D

Tredewe

The Bowling Green

I grid square represents 500 metres

Messack

Trelissa

E   F   **35**   G   H

I

Tregairewoon
Farm

2

A3078

Lanhoose

3

44

Trewithian

Pollaughan

Hotel
4

Rosevine

Trethem
Mill

Hotel

5

E   F   **51**   G   Tregassa   H   Porthcurnick
Beach

Lanhay

Portscatho

44

Treworthal

A

B

36 worlas

C

D

1

Treluggan

Rocky Lane

Pendower Beach

A3078

2

Curgurrell

3

Creek Stephen Point

43

ewithian

South West Coast Path

4

Hotel

Rosevine

Hotel

5

A

B

C

D

Porthcurnick Beach

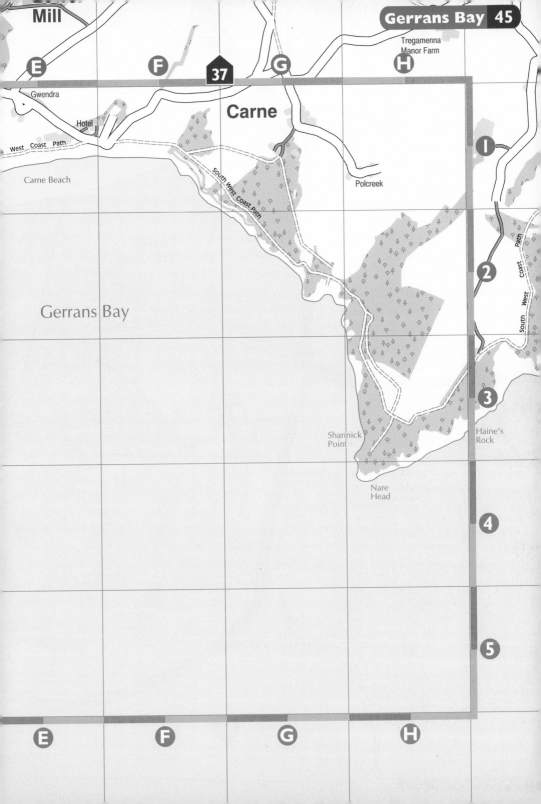

Mill

Tregamenna
Manor Farm

E

F

37

G

H

Gwendra

Carne

Hotel

West Coast Path

I

Carne Beach

South West Coast Path

Polcreek

2

Gerrans Bay

South West Coast Path

3

Shannick
Point

Haine's
Rock

Nare
Head

4

5

E

F

G

H

A5
1 Spargo Ct

A4
1 Carnsew Crs
2 Penvean Cl

A **B** 38 **C** **D**

Roskrow

I

D3
1 Andrewartha Rd
2 Dunvegan Rd
3 Green Lane Cl
4 Harbour Vw
5 Parc-an-Challow
6 Trekeen Rd
7 Western Pl

Lower
Treluswell

Lanoweth

2

Packsaddle
Close
Bodinar

D4
1 Fairmeadow
2 Polwithen Rd
3 Woodside

Treliever

Trevarton
Road

A39

Packsaddle

Treliever Rd

4
2

A394

West
Indu
Est

3

Glen
Vw

Greenwood Road

Penvale Dr

Highland Dr

Penryn
Station

D5
1 Woodway

Tremough

Treverbyn
Treyanve

Greenwood Crs

Penvale Crescent

Pentire
Road

Green

6
5 **3**

TR10

Carnsew
Farm

Lanaton
Road

Junior &
Infant School

2

4

Carnsew
Close

Mabe County
Primary School

Park

Penryn
Community
School

Poltisko Rd

Poltisko Ter

1

Kernick

Gweal
Darras

Cunningham

Treliever Road

Summerheath

1

Parkengue

Penryn
Rugby
Club

Woodland
Rd

Poltair
Road

Pols

PO

Antron Hill

Antron Hill

Kernick Road

Annear
Road

Ltl
Oaks

Woodland Av

Wood V

2

Antron Way

Jennings Rd

Kernick
Business Park

Oaks Cl

Gills Cl

5

Efron Cl

1

Mabe
Burnthouse

Kernick
House

Church Road

Antron 1a

Antron
Farm

Lane

A **B** College
Reservoir 52 **C** **D**

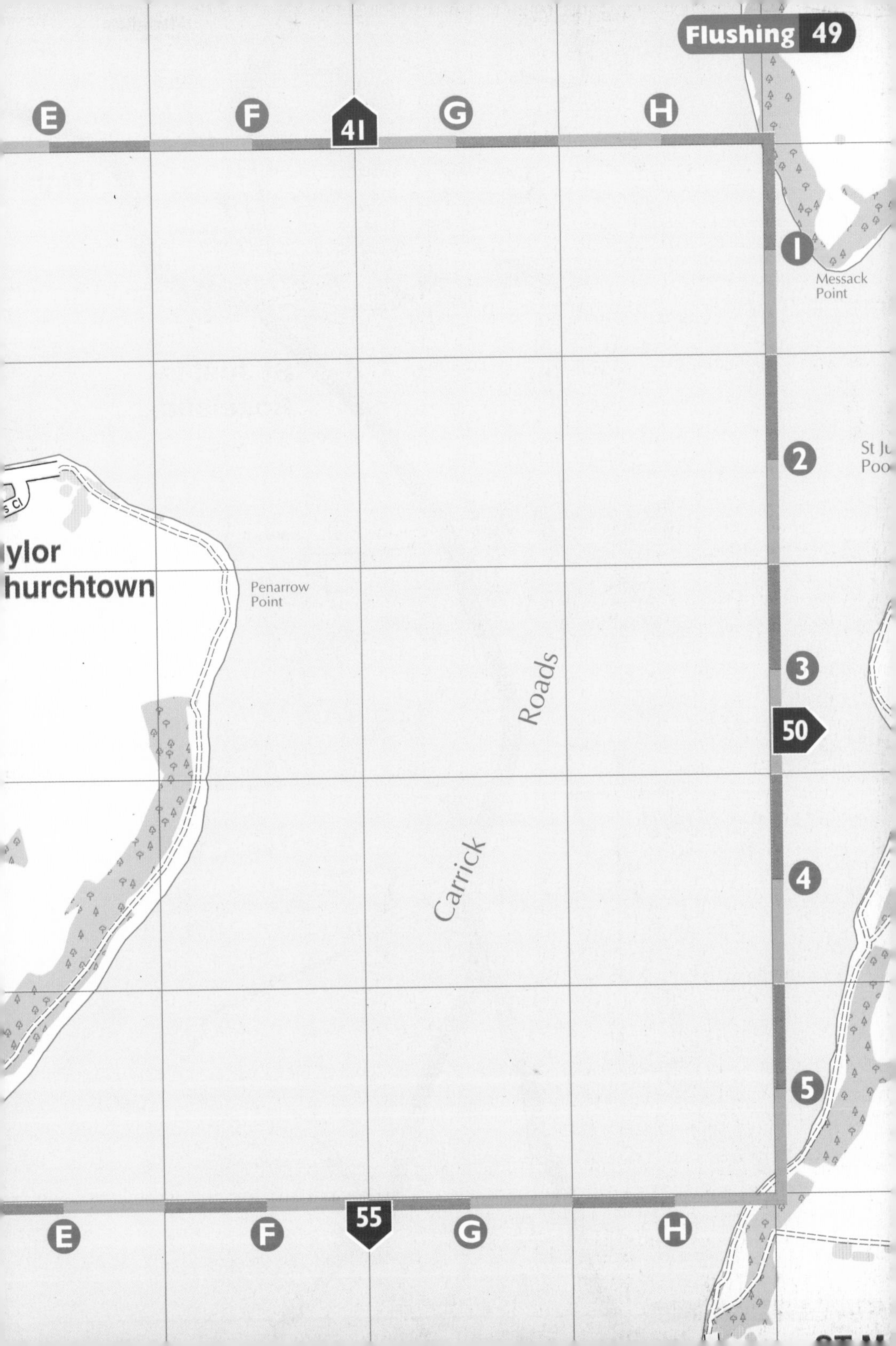

E F **41** G H

I

Messack
Point

2 St Ju
Poo

3

50

4

5

E F **55** G H

ylor
hurchtown

Penarrow
Point

Roads

Carrick

ST M

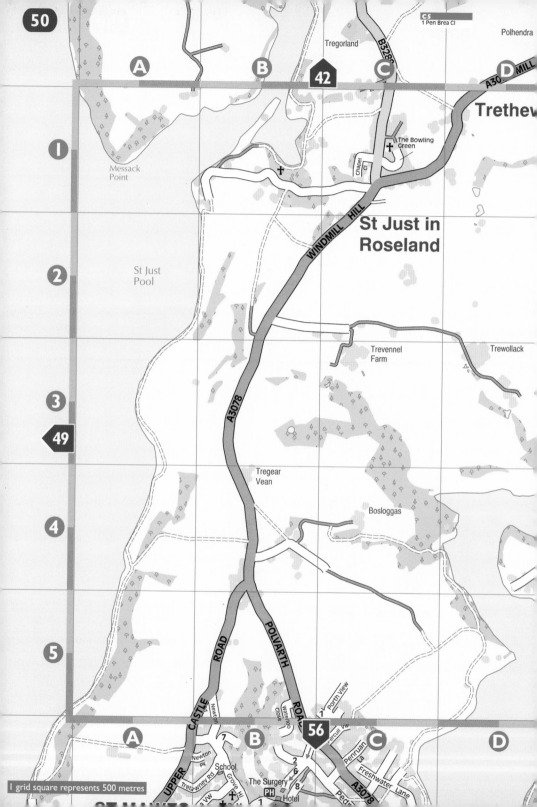

Ⓐ   Ⓑ   **42**   Ⓒ   Ⓓ

C5
1 Pen Brea Cl

Polhendra

Tregorland

B3289

A30 MILL

Trethew

The Bowling
Green

Chapel
Cl

Ⅰ

Messack
Point

WINDMILL HILL

**St Just in
Roseland**

2

St Just
Pool

Trevennel
Farm

Trewollack

3

A3078

49

Tregear
Vean

4

Bosloggas

5

CASTLE ROAD

NEWTON

POLVARTH ROAD

Waterloo
Close

Porth View

Penruan La

Freshwater Lane

56

A3078

Ⓐ   Ⓑ   **56**   Ⓒ   Ⓓ

UPPER

Newton
Pk

School

Trelawney Rd

Grove Hl

The Surgery

PH

Hotel

ST MAWES

G2 1 Treventon Cl

H2 1 Parc Merys

Mill

E   F   **43**   G   H

Tregassa

Lanhay

Tregassa

Portscatho

Porthcurnick Beach

1

Parc-An-Dillon Rd

Treventon Rd

Churchtown Road

North Parade

Gerrans

1

1

River St

PO

The Square

2

Gerrans Square

✝

Gerrans Hill

The Lugger

Pencabe

The Surgery

Treloan

Gerrans Primary School

Treloan Lane

3

Tregassick

Treloan

Tregassick Road

Percuil River

South West Coast Path

4

rcuil

5

Trewince

Greeb Point

E   F   **57**   G   H

Froe

Rosteague

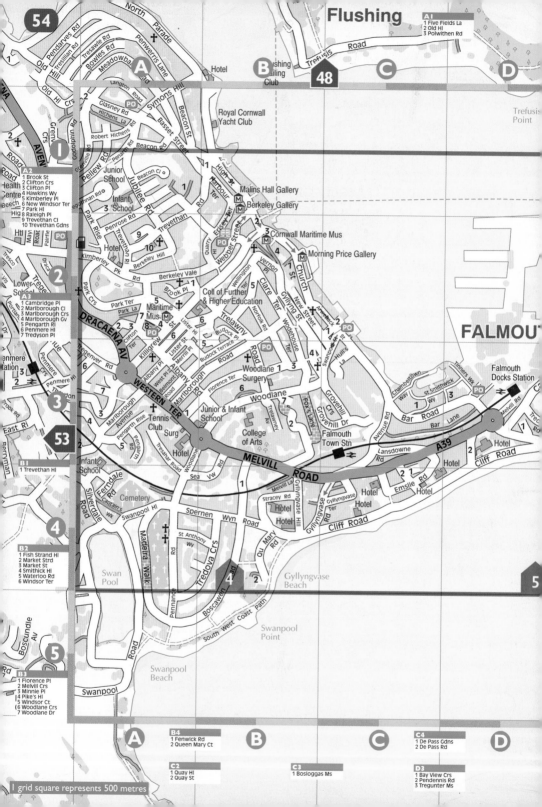

54

48

FALMOUT

Falmouth Docks Station

53

5

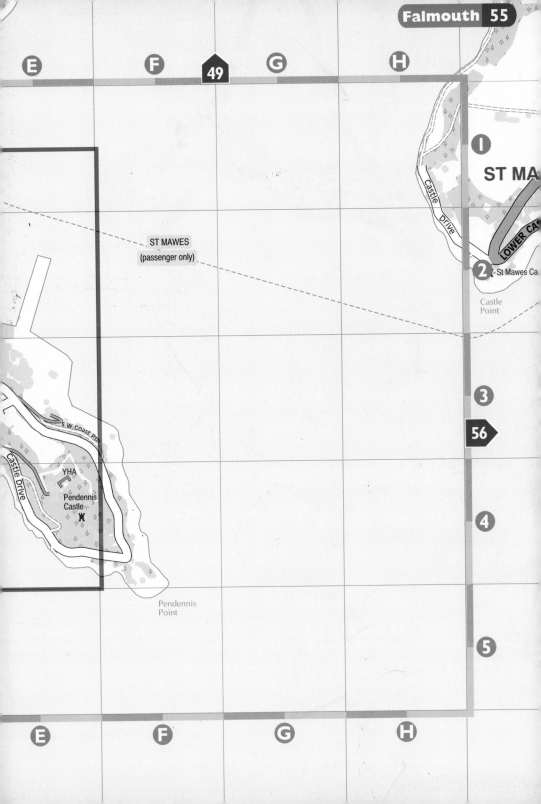

E F **49** G H

I

ST MA

Castle Drive

LOWER CA

2 St Mawes Ca

Castle Point

3

56

4

S.W. Coast Path

Castle Drive

YHA

Pendennis Castle

Pendennis Point

5

ST MAWES
(passenger only)

E F G H

B1
1 Trevethan Hl

A   B   50   C   D

50

orth View

Waterloo Close

Percull Vw

Penruan La

Freshwater Lane

UPPER CASTLE ROAD

CASTLE ROAD

VARTH ROAD

1

Newton PK

7

School

Trelawney Rd

Grove H

2
6

8

The Surgery

PH

Hotel

A3078

Pedn-Moran

ST MAWES

Sea Vw Crs

† St Mawes

Sailing
Club

3

7

KINGS ROAD

Hotel

TREDENHAM ROAD

Buckeys La

Riviera La

4

5

THE QUAY

†

PO

LOWER CASTLE RD   MARINE PARADE

St Mawes
Harbour

2   ⛫ St Mawes Castle

FALMOUTH
(passenger only)

Castle
Point

Castle Drive

I

3

55

Carricknath
Point

Place
House

†

St
Anthony

4

Place
Barton

Military Road

5

St Anthony
Head

South West Coast Path

A   B   C   Zone
Point   D

I grid square represents 500 metres

Trewince

E

F

51

Rostea

G

Greeb Point

H

Froe

I

South West Coast Path

Porth Farm

2

Bohortha

Killigerran Head

3

Porthmellin Head

Porthbeor Beach

4

5

E

F

G

H

Angarrick 39 H3	Goon Piper 33 E4	Mylor Churchtown 48 C2	St Anthony
Baldhu 22 D2	Green Bottom 14 B2	Newbridge 15 H4	St Clement
Bissoe 22 C5	Greenwith Common 30 C2	New Mill 16 B1	St Gluvias
Bissom 47 G3	Harcourt 40 D2	Old Kea 26 B4	St Just in Roseland
Bohortha 57 E3	Helston Water 23 E5	Parkengear 13 E3	St Mawes
Boslowick 53 H4	Hick's Mill 30 B1	Penelewey 32 D1	St Micheal Penkevil
Budock Water 52 D3	Hightown 16 A4	Penpol 32 C4	Shortlanesend
Burnthouse 38 A4	Higher Trevilla 33 F4	Penryn 47 E3	Threemilestone
Calenick 24 D2	Hugus 14 D5	Penweathers 16 A5	Tomperrow
Carclew 39 F2	Idless 9 E3	Percuil 51 E4	Tregew
Carne 45 G1	Kea 24 C2	Perranarworthal 30 B5	Trelew
Carnon Downs 31 G2	Kenwyn 16 D1	Perranwell 30 C4	Treliske
Chycoose 32 B4	Kerley Downs 14 A5	Perranwell Station 31 E3	Trelissick
Come-to-Good 32 D2	Lamanva 52 B4	Perran Wharf 31 E5	Tresawle
Coombe 25 G5	Lamorran 27 H4	Philleigh 35 G3	Tresillian
Coombe 30 A1	Lower Mill 37 E5	Playing Place 24 D4	Trethewell
Cowlands 33 F1	Lower Treluswell 46 C2	Point 32 C5	Trewarthenick
Curgurrell 44 A2	Lower Trevilla 33 F5	Porth Kea 25 F4	Trewithian
Cusveorth Coombe 22 B2	Mabe Burnthouse 46 B5	Portscatho 51 G1	Treworga
Devoran 31 H4	Malpas 26 A2	Probus 12 D2	Treworlas
Falmouth 5 G3	Melinsey 37 F4	Restronguet Passage 40 B3	Treworthal
Feock 41 E1	Merther 18 D4	Rosevine 43 H5	Truro
Flushing 48 C5	Merther Lane 27 E2	Roseworthy 7 G3	Twelveheads
Gerrans 51 F2	Mongleath 53 G2	Ruan High Lanes 37 E3	Veryan
Gloweth 15 G3	Mylor Bridge 40 A4	Ruan Lanihorne 28 D3	Wheal Baddon

USING THE STREET INDEX

Street names are listed alphabetically. Each street name is followed by its postal town or area locality, the Postcode District, the page number, and the reference to the square in which the name is found.

Example: **Agar Mdw** *RTRUS* TR3.....................**31 H2** 🔲

Some entries are followed by a number in a blue box. This number indicates the location of the street within the referenced grid square. The full street name is listed at the side of the map page.

GENERAL ABBREVIATIONS

ACC .... ACCESS	EMB .... EMBANKMENT	LK .... LOCK	RDG .... RID
ALY .... ALLEY	EMBY .... EMBASSY	LKS .... LAKES	REP .... REPUE
AP .... APPROACH	ESP .... ESPLANADE	LNDG .... LANDING	RES .... RESERV
AR .... ARCADE	EST .... ESTATE	LTL .... LITTLE	RFC .... RUGBY FOOTBALL CI
ASS .... ASSOCIATION	EX .... EXCHANGE	LWR .... LOWER	RI .... F
AV .... AVENUE	EXPY .... EXPRESSWAY	MAG .... MAGISTRATE	RP .... RA
BCH .... BEACH	EXT .... EXTENSION	MAN .... MANSIONS	RW .... R
BLDS .... BUILDINGS	F/O .... FLYOVER	MD .... MEAD	S .... SOL
BND .... BEND	FC .... FOOTBALL CLUB	MDW .... MEADOWS	SCH .... SCHC
BNK .... BANK	FK .... FORK	MEM .... MEMORIAL	SE .... SOUTH E/
BR .... BRIDGE	FLD .... FIELD	MKT .... MARKET	SER .... SERVICE AF
BRK .... BROOK	FLDS .... FIELDS	MKTS .... MARKETS	SH .... SHC
BTM .... BOTTOM	FLS .... FALLS	ML .... MALL	SHOP .... SHOPPI
BUS .... BUSINESS	FLS .... FLATS	ML .... MILL	SKWY .... SKYW
BVD .... BOULEVARD	FM .... FARM	MNR .... MANOR	SMT .... SUMI
BY .... BYPASS	FT .... FORT	MS .... MEWS	SOC .... SOCIE
CATH .... CATHEDRAL	FWY .... FREEWAY	MSN .... MISSION	SP .... SP
CEM .... CEMETERY	FY .... FERRY	MT .... MOUNT	SPR .... SPRI
CEN .... CENTRE	GA .... GATE	MTN .... MOUNTAIN	SQ .... SQUA
CFT .... CROFT	GAL .... GALLERY	MTS .... MOUNTAINS	ST .... STRE
CH .... CHURCH	GDN .... GARDEN	MUS .... MUSEUM	STN .... STATI
CHA .... CHASE	GDNS .... GARDENS	MWY .... MOTORWAY	STR .... STRE
CHYD .... CHURCHYARD	GLD .... GLADE	N .... N	STRD .... STRA
CIR .... CIRCLE	GLN .... GLEN	NE .... NORTH EAST	SW .... SOUTH WE
CIRC .... CIRCUS	GN .... GREEN	NW .... NORTH WEST	TDG .... TRADI
CL .... CLOSE	GND .... GROUND	O/P .... OVERPASS	TER .... TERRA
CLFS .... CLIFFS	GRA .... GRANGE	OFF .... OFFICE	THWY .... THROUGHW
CMP .... CAMP	GRG .... GARAGE	ORCH .... ORCHARD	TNL .... TUNN
CNR .... CORNER	GT .... GREAT	OV .... OVAL	TOLL .... TOLLW
CO .... COUNTY	GTWY .... GATEWAY	PAL .... PALACE	TPK .... TURNPI
COLL .... COLLEGE	GV .... GROVE	PAS .... PASSAGE	TR .... TRA
COM .... COMMON	HGR .... HIGHER	PAV .... PAVILION	TRL .... TR/
COMM .... COMMISSION	HL .... HILL	PDE .... PARADE	TWR .... TOW
CON .... CONVENT	HLS .... HILLS	PH .... PUBLIC HOUSE	U/P .... UNDERPA
COT .... COTTAGE	HO .... HOUSE	PK .... PARK	UNI .... UNIVERS
COTS .... COTTAGES	HOL .... HOLLOW	PKWY .... PARKWAY	UPR .... UPP
CP .... CAPE	HOSP .... HOSPITAL	PL .... PLACE	V .... VA
CPS .... COPSE	HRB .... HARBOUR	PLN .... PLAIN	VA .... VALL
CR .... CREEK	HTH .... HEATH	PLNS .... PLAINS	VIAD .... VIADU
CREM .... CREMATORIUM	HTS .... HEIGHTS	PLZ .... PLAZA	VIL VIL
CRS .... CRESCENT	HVN .... HAVEN	POL .... POLICE STATION	VIS .... VIS
CSWY .... CAUSEWAY	HWY .... HIGHWAY	PR .... PRINCE	VLG .... VILLA
CT .... COURT	IMP .... IMPERIAL	PREC .... PRECINCT	VLS VILL
CTRL .... CENTRAL	IN .... INLET	PREP .... PREPARATORY	VW .... VIE
CTS .... COURTS	IND EST .... INDUSTRIAL ESTATE	PRIM .... PRIMARY	W .... W
CTYD .... COURTYARD	INF .... INFIRMARY	PROM .... PROMENADE	WD .... WOO
CUTT .... CUTTINGS	INFO .... INFORMATION	PRS .... PRINCESS	WHF .... WHAF
CV .... COVE	INT .... INTERCHANGE	PRT .... PORT	WK .... WA
CYN .... CANYON	IS .... ISLAND	PT .... POINT	WKS .... WAL
DEPT .... DEPARTMENT	JCT .... JUNCTION	PTH .... PATH	WLS .... WEL
DL .... DALE	JTY .... JETTY	PZ .... PIAZZA	WY .... W
DM .... DAM	KG .... KING	QD .... QUADRANT	YD .... YAF
DR .... DRIVE	KNL .... KNOLL	QU .... QUEEN	YHA .... YOUTH HOST
DRO .... DROVE	L .... LAKE	QY .... QUAY	
DRY .... DRIVEWAY	LA .... LANE	R .... RIVER	
DWGS .... DWELLINGS	LDG .... LODGE	RBT .... ROUNDABOUT	
E .... EAST	LGT .... LIGHT	RD .... ROAD	

STCODE TOWNS AND AREA ABBREVIATIONS

...................................Falmouth   RTRUE/STMW ..Rural Truro east/St Mawes   RTRUS ....Rural Truro south   TRU..................................Truro
YN ....Penryn   RTRUNW..............Rural Truro north & west

ndex - streets

Aca - Gle

A

a Rd *FAL* TR11 .... 53 H1
Ct *TRU* TR1 .... 3 H3
Mdw *RTRUS* TR3 .... 31 H2 ⓘ
Rd *TRU* TR1 .... 3 H3
y Pl *FAL* TR11 .... 4 B4
y Rd *FAL* TR11 .... 4 B4
J TR1 .... 2 A4
t Pl *TRU* TR1 .... 2 E6
Rd *TRU* TR1 .... 16 B3
J TR1 .... 3 J2
ton Ct *TRU* TR1 .... 3 H3
ton Ter *TRU* TR1 .... 3 H3
ia Cl *RTRUE/STMW* TR2 .... 12 D2
ewartha Rd
NRYN TR10 .... 46 D3 ⓘ
ew Pl *TRU* TR1 .... 2 E4
ar Rd *PENRYN* TR10 .... 46 C5
on La *PENRYN* TR10............... 46 A5
on Wy *PENRYN* TR10 .... 46 A5
HI *TRU* TR1 .... 16 D5
eim Ter *FAL* TR11 .... 48 B4 ⓘ
dell Pl *TRU* TR1 .... 3 F7
enack St *FAL* TR11 .... 4 D3
orthal Mdw *RTRUS* TR3 .... 30 D4
ield Rd *FAL* TR11 .... 47 H5
eigh Wy
RUE/STMW TR2 .... 13 E2 ⓘ
ey Rd *RTRUNW* TR4 .... 8 B2
U TR1 .... 2 E5
Rd *FAL* TR11 .... 4 E6
Avenue *TRU* TR1 .... 3 H3
dale Rd *TRU* TR1 .... 2 C4

B

k La *RTRUE/STMW* TR2 .... 37 H3
k Quay *TRU* TR1 .... 3 G5
La *FAL* TR11 .... 5 F5
ack La *FAL* TR11 .... 3 F6
Rd *FAL* TR11 .... 5 F5
ton Meadow *TRU* TR1................. 2 B3
set St *FAL* TR11 .... 54 A1
View Crs *FAL* TR11 .... 5 F5
con Cl *FAL* TR11 .... 4 A1
con St *FAL* TR11 .... 54 A1
con St *FAL* TR11 .... 54 A1
ruthan Av *TRU* TR1 .... 3 K1
ch Cl *FAL* TR11 .... 53 H1
ch Cl *FAL* TR11 .... 53 H1 ⓘ
enna Dr *TRU* TR1 .... 16 B3
nay *PENRYN* TR10 .... 47 E3
's HI *FAL* TR11 .... 40 A4
mont Rd *FAL* TR11 .... 4 B4
mont Ter *RTRUS* TR3 .... 31 G4
son Rd *TRU* TR1 .... 2 D3
keley HI *FAL* TR11 .... 4 A2
kele V *FAL* TR11 .... 4 B3
ryman Crs *FAL* TR11 .... 53 H3
veth Cl *RTRUS* TR5 .... 15 E3 ⓘ
kland HI *FAL* TR11 .... 53 E2
kland Water Rd *FAL* TR11 ..... 53 F2
ops Cl *TRU* TR1 .... 17 E1
soe Rd *RTRUS* TR3 .... 31 G1
som Rd *PENRYN* TR10 .... 47 E3
soe Rd *RTRUS* TR3 .... 31 G1 ⓘ
dinar Rd *PENRYN* TR10 .... 46 C2
dmin Rd *TRU* TR1 .... 3 J1
nelland Ri *PENRYN* TR10 .... 47 F3
nelland Rd *PENRYN* TR10 ..... 47 F3
nelland Wy *PENRYN* TR10 ..... 47 F3
nella Rd *RTRUE/STMW* TR2 .. 56 B1 ⓘ
nill *PENRYN* TR10 .... 47 F4
nython Cl *FAL* TR11 .... 40 B5
scawen Rd *FAL* TR11 .... 4 C7
scawen St *TRU* TR1 .... 3 G4
scundle Av *FAL* TR11 .... 53 H5

C

Calenick St *TRU* TR1 .... 3 F5
Cambridge Pl *FAL* TR11 .... 4 B5
Campfield HI *TRU* TR1 .... 3 G3
Captain's Wk *FAL* TR11 .... 4 A4
Carclew Rd *FAL* TR11 .... 39 G2
Carclew St *TRU* TR1 .... 3 G5
Carclew Ter *RTRUS* TR3 .... 31 G4
Carew-Pole Cl *TRU* TR1 .... 3 J7
Carew St *TRU* TR1 .... 2 E3
Carey Pk *TRU* TR1 .... 2 E5
Carlyon Cl *RTRUS* TR3 .... 15 E3 ⓘ
Carlyon Rd *RTRUS* TR3 .... 24 C4
TRU TR1 .... 2 D2
Carne Mdw *RTRUE/STMW* TR2 .. 11 E5
Carne View Rd
RTRUE/STMW TR2 .... 13 E2
Carnon Crs *RTRUS* TR3 .... 31 H2 ⓘ
Carnon Ter *RTRUS* TR3 .... 31 G4 ⓘ
Carnsew Cl *RTRUS* TR3.............. 46 A4
Carnsew Crs *PENRYN* TR10 .. 46 A4 ⓘ
Carrick Rd *FAL* TR11 .... 53 G4
Carrick Wy *RTRUE/STMW* TR2 .. 56 B1 ⓘ
Carrine Rd *FAL* TR11 .... 16 A4
Carvoza Rd *TRU* TR1 .... 3 H3
Castle Cl *FAL* TR11 .... 5 J5
Castle Dr *FAL* TR11 .... 5 K5
Castle Ri *FAL* TR11 .... 2 E3
Castle Rd *FAL* TR11 .... 3 F4
Castle Ri *RTRUE/STMW* TR2 ...... 55 H1
The Causeway *FAL* TR11 .... 53 H2
Century La *RTRUE/STMW* TR2 .. 37 H4
Chainwalk Dr *TRU* TR1 .... 2 D2
Chapel Cl *RTRUE/STMW* TR2 .. 50 C1
Chapel HI *TRU* TR1 .... 2 C5
Chapel La *PENRYN* TR10 .... 47 E4
Chapel Rw *TRU* TR1 .... 3 F6
Chapel St *RTRUE/STMW* TR2 .... 12 D1
Chapel Ter *RTRUE/STMW* TR2 .... 56 B1 ⓘ
RTRUS TR3 .... 31 H4 ⓘ
Charles Av *FAL* TR11 .... 53 G4
Charles St *TRU* TR1 .... 3 G4
Charter Ct *PENRYN* TR10 .... 47 F4 ⓘ
Chellew Rd *TRU* TR1 .... 3 K3
Chestnut Cl *FAL* TR11 .... 53 H1
Chirgwin Rd *TRU* TR1 .... 3 K4
Church HI *PENRYN* TR10 .... 47 F3
RTRUE/STMW TR2 .... 56 B1 ⓘ
Church La *FAL* TR11 .... 48 B4 ⓘ
Church Rd *FAL* TR11 .... 48 B1
PENRYN TR10 .... 47 F4
PENRYN TR10 .... 52 A1
RTRUNW TR4 .... 8 B2
RTRUS TR3 .... 30 D5

Church St / D column

Church St *FAL* TR11 .... 4 D2
Church Ter *RTRUS* TR3 .... 31 G4 ⓘ
Churchtown Rd
RTRUE/STMW TR2 .... 51 G2
Church View Rd
RTRUE/STMW TR2 .... 13 E2 ⓘ
Church Wy *FAL* TR11 .... 4 D2
Chycoose Parc *RTRUS* TR3.......... 32 B5
Chyreen La *RTRUS* TR3 .... 23 G5
Chyvelah Ope *RTRUS* TR3 ...... 15 G3 ⓘ
Chyvelah Rd *RTRUS* TR3 .... 14 D2
Chyvelah V *RTRUS* TR3 .... 15 G3
City Rd *TRU* TR1 .... 2 E5
Clare Ter *FAL* TR11 .... 4 C3
Cliff Rd *FAL* TR11 .... 4 E6
Clifton Crs *FAL* TR11 .... 4 A3
Clifton Pl *FAL* TR11 .... 4 A3 ⓘ
Clifton Ter *FAL* TR11 .... 4 A4
The Close *FAL* TR11 .... 40 A4
TRU TR1 .... 17 H1
Cogos Pk *FAL* TR11 .... 40 A5
Coldrose Ct *TRU* TR1 .... 2 C5 ⓘ
College Rd *RTRUE/STMW* TR2 .. 12 C2
College HI *PENRYN* TR10 .... 47 F4
Colworth Av *FAL* TR11 .... 53 H3 ⓘ
Comfort Rd *FAL* TR11 .... 40 A5
Commercial Rd *PENRYN* TR10... 47 F3
RTRUE/STMW TR2 .... 56 B1 ⓘ
Comprigney Cl *TRU* TR1 .... 2 D2 ⓘ
Comprigney HI *TRU* TR1 .... 2 C2
Conway Cl *FAL* TR11 .... 53 G2 ⓘ
Conway Gdns *FAL* TR11 .... 53 F2
Conway Rd *FAL* TR11 .... 53 F1
Coombe La *RTRUNW* TR4 .... 30 A1
Coosebean La *TRU* TR1 .... 2 A2
Copes Gdns *TRU* TR1 .... 3 F2
Cornish Crs *TRU* TR1 .... 16 B2
Cornubia Cl *TRU* TR1 .... 3 K1
Cornwall County
PENRYN TR10 .... 47 E3 ⓘ
Cotsland Rd *TRU* TR1 .... 17 H2
Courtney Rd *TRU* TR1 .... 2 D3
Cove HI *RTRUS* TR3 .... 30 C5
Coventry Rd *FAL* TR11 .... 48 B5
Cowling Rd *RTRUS* TR3 .... 31 H1 ⓘ
Creekside Vw *RTRUE/STMW* TR2 .. 19 E1
Crescent Gdns *TRU* TR1 .... 2 C4
Crescent Ri *TRU* TR1 .... 2 C5
Crescent Rd *TRU* TR1 .... 2 D5
The Crescent *TRU* TR1 .... 2 C4
Crossways *FAL* TR11 .... 53 H4 ⓘ
Cryon Vw *TRU* TR1 .... 15 H3
Cullen Vw *RTRUE/STMW* TR2..... 12 D2
Cunningham Pk *PENRYN* TR10 .. 46 B4
Cyril Rd *TRU* TR1 .... 2 E2

D

Daniell Ct *TRU* TR1 .... 2 E7
Daniell Rd *TRU* TR1 .... 2 D7
Daniell St *TRU* TR1 .... 2 E6
Daubuz Cl *TRU* TR1 .... 3 F1
Daubuz Ct *TRU* TR1 .... 3 F3
Davey's Cl *FAL* TR11 .... 53 G5
David Penhaligon Wy *TRU* 3 G6
Deeble Cl *RTRUS* TR3 .... 14 D3 ⓘ
Denas Water *RTRUE/STMW* TR2 ... 11 G4
De Pass Gdns *FAL* TR11 .... 5 F6
De Pass Rd *FAL* TR11 .... 5 F6
Devoran La *RTRUS* TR3 .... 31 G4
Diana Cl *FAL* TR11 .... 53 G4 ⓘ
Dicky La *RTRUS* TR3................... 33 H3
Dobbs La *TRU* TR1 .... 2 B4
Dozmere *RTRUS* TR3 .... 32 D5
Dozmere Cl *RTRUS* TR3 .... 33 E5 ⓘ
Dracaena Av *FAL* TR11 .... 4 A4
FAL TR11.................................... 47 H5
Dracaena Pl *FAL* TR11 .... 53 H2
Dudman Rd *TRU* TR1 .... 16 B3
Duncannon Dr *FAL* TR11............ 53 H2
Dunstan Cl *PENRYN* TR10 ..... 47 E3 ⓘ

E

Dunvegan Rd *PENRYN* TR10 ..... 46 D3 ⓘ
Durgan La *PENRYN* TR10 .... 47 E3

E

East Ri *FAL* TR11 .... 53 H3
Eastwood Rd *PENRYN* TR10 ..... 47 F4
Edwards Rd *RTRUS* TR3 .... 31 G4
Edward St *TRU* TR1 .... 3 F4
Eglos Meadow *FAL* TR11 .... 40 A4 ⓘ
Eglos Rd *RTRUNW* TR4 .... 8 B2
Elerkey Cl *RTRUE/STMW* TR2 .... 37 G3 ⓘ
Elerkey La *RTRUE/STMW* TR2 ... 37 G4
Eliot Rd *TRU* TR1 .... 2 E2
Elizabeth Cl *RTRUS* TR3 .... 14 D3 ⓘ
Elm Ct *TRU* TR1 .... 3 G2
Elm Court Gdns *TRU* TR1 .... 3 G5 ⓘ
Elm Dr *RTRUS* TR3 .... 33 E5
Elm Gv *RTRUS* TR3 .... 41 E1
Elm Meadow *RTRUS* TR3 .... 41 E1 ⓘ
Elowen Cl *FAL* TR11 .... 53 G4
Empire Wy *FAL* TR11 .... 53 F2
Emslie Rd *FAL* TR11 .... 5 F6
Enys Cl *TRU* TR1 .... 2 D2
Enys Rd *TRU* TR1 .... 2 D2
Epworth Ct *TRU* TR1 .... 3 J5
Erisey Ter *FAL* TR11 .... 4 C2
Erow Glas *PENRYN* TR10 .... 47 E3 ⓘ
Esperanza Ct *FAL* TR11 .... 47 H5 ⓘ
Eston Cl *PENRYN* TR10 .... 46 A5
Evea Cl *TRU* TR1 .... 16 A4

F

Fairfax Rd *RTRUE/STMW* TR2 .... 11 F4
Fairfield Rd *FAL* TR11 .... 53 H2
Fairmantle St *TRU* TR1 .... 3 G5
Fairmeadow *PENRYN* TR10 ..... 46 D4 ⓘ
Falmouth Rd *FAL* TR11 .... 47 G5
PENRYN TR10 .... 47 G4
TRU TR1 .... 3 F7
Faulkener Cl *FAL* TR11 .... 53 G2
Fenwick Rd *FAL* TR11 .... 4 C6
Ferndale Rd *FAL* TR11 .... 4 A4
Ferris Town *TRU* TR1 .... 2 E4
Fish Strand HI *FAL* TR11 .... 4 D2 ⓘ
Five Fields La *FAL* TR11 .... 4 B1
Florence Pl *FAL* TR11 .... 4 D4
Florence Ter *FAL* TR11 .... 4 C4
Fore St *RTRUE/STMW* TR2 .... 12 C2
The Forge *RTRUS* TR3 .... 32 A1
Forge Wy *RTRUNW* TR4 .... 8 B2
Forth Coth *RTRUS* TR3 .... 31 H2
Forth Noweth *RTRUS* TR3 .... 31 H1
Four Acres Rd *RTRUE/STMW* TR2 .. 37 G4
Fox's La *FAL* TR11 .... 4 D4
Foxstanton Dr *PENRYN* TR10 .. 47 F4 ⓘ
Frances St *TRU* TR1 .... 2 E4
Frankland Cl *FAL* TR11 .... 53 H3 ⓘ
Freshwater La *RTRUE/STMW* TR2.. 56 C1
Frost Ct *FAL* TR11 .... 53 G1 ⓘ

G

Galland Rd *TRU* TR1 .... 16 B2 ⓘ
Ganges Cl *FAL* TR11 .... 49 E2
Garden Meadow *FAL* TR11 ...... 53 G3 ⓘ
Gas HI *TRU* TR1 .... 17 G5
George St *TRU* TR1 .... 3 F4
Gerrans HI *RTRUE/STMW* TR2 .. 51 G2
Gerrans Sq *RTRUE/STMW* TR2 .. 51 G2
Gig La *RTRUS* TR3 .... 32 A2
Gills Ct *PENRYN* TR10 .... 46 D5
Glasney Pl *PENRYN* TR10 .... 47 F4
Glasney Rd *FAL* TR11 .... 54 A1
Glasney Ter *PENRYN* TR10 .... 47 F4
Glenthorne Rd *RTRUS* TR3 ...... 14 D3

Glen Vw *PENRYN* TR10 .... 46 D3
Gloweth Vw *TRU* TR1 .... 15 H3
The Gluyas *FAL* TR11 .... 53 G5
Glyn Wy *RTRUS* TR3.......................... 15 E3
Godolphin Rd *FAL* TR11 .... 53 H1
Goonvrea *RTRUS* TR3 .... 38 C1
Greenbank Rd *RTRUS* TR3 .... 31 G4
Green Cl *RTRUS* TR3.......................... 41 E1
   TRU TR1 .... 2 D7
Green La *PENRYN* TR10...................... 46 D3
   RTRUE/STMW TR2 .... 37 H3
   TRU TR1 .... 2 C6
Green Lane Cl *PENRYN* TR10 .. 46 D3 ▣
Green St *TRU* TR1.............................. 3 H5
Greenwith Cl *TRU* TR1 .... 2 D6 ▣
Greenwith Hl *RTRUS* TR3 .... 30 C3
Greenwith Rd *RTRUS* TR3.................. 30 C3
Greenwood Crs *PENRYN* TR10.......... 46 C3
Greenwood Rd *PENRYN* TR10 .... 46 C3
Grenna La *RTRUS* TR3 .... 31 E1
Grenville Crs *FAL* TR11 .... 53 H1
Grenville Rd *FAL* TR11 .... 53 H1
   TRU TR1 .... 2 D2
Grove Hl *RTRUE/STMW* TR2 .... 56 B1
Grovehill Crs *FAL* TR11 .... 4 E4
Grovehill Dr *FAL* TR11 .... 4 D5
Gwarnick Rd *TRU* TR1 .... 2 D5
Gweal Darras *PENRYN* TR10 .... 46 A4
Gwel-an-scol *RTRUS* TR3 .... 33 E5 ▣
Gwell-an-nans *RTRUE/STMW* TR2.. 12 D2
Gwendroc Cl *TRU* TR1 .... 3 G7
Gyllyng St *FAL* TR11.......................... 4 D3
Gyllyngvase Hl *FAL* TR11 .... 4 D6
Gyllyngvase Rd *FAL* TR11 .... 4 E6
Gyllyngvase Ter *FAL* TR11................. 4 E6

H

Halvarras Pk *RTRUS* TR3.................. 24 C5
Halvarras Rd *RTRUS* TR3 .... 24 C5
Halwyn Pl *TRU* TR1 .... 2 D5
Harbour Ter *FAL* TR11 .... 4 C1
Harbour Vw *PENRYN* TR10 .... 46 D3 ▣
   TRU TR1 .... 3 K7
Harcourt Cl *TRU* TR1 .... 16 B3 ▣
Harvey Rd *TRU* TR1 .... 17 F5
Hawkins Wy *FAL* TR11....................... 4 B3
Hawthorn Wy *RTRUS* TR3 .... 14 D3 ▣
Hayne Corfe Gdns *TRU* TR1 .... 2 A4 ▣
Helston Rd *PENRYN* TR10................. 47 E3
Hendra Barton *TRU* TR1 .... 2 D2
Hendra La *TRU* TR1 .... 2 E3
Hendra Rd *TRU* TR1 .... 2 D2
Hendra Vean *TRU* TR1 .... 2 D2
Heron Cl *RTRUE/STMW* TR2 .... 11 F5
Heron Wy *TRU* TR1 .... 25 G1
Hichens La *FAL* TR11 .... 54 A1
Hicks Cl *RTRUE/STMW* TR2.............. 12 D2
High Cross *TRU* TR1 .... 3 G4
Higher Market St
   PENRYN TR10 .... 47 F4 ▣
Higher Newham La *TRU* TR1 .... 17 F5
Higher Polsue Wy
   RTRUE/STMW TR2 .... 11 E5
Higher Redannick *TRU* TR1 .... 2 D6
Hightertown *TRU* TR1 .... 16 B3
Higher Trehaverne *TRU* TR1 .... 2 E2
Highfield Rd *FAL* TR11....................... 53 H2
Highland Pk *PENRYN* TR10................ 46 D3
High St *FAL* TR11 .... 4 C1
   RTRUE/STMW TR2 .... 12 D2
Hillcrest *RTRUNW* TR4........................ 8 B2
Hillcrest Av *TRU* TR1 .... 2 B3
Hill Head *PENRYN* TR10..................... 47 F5
Hillhead Av *RTRUE/STMW* TR2 .. 56 B1 ▣
Hillhead Rd *FAL* TR11 .... 52 D1
Hillside Meadow
   PENRYN TR10 .... 47 F4 ▣
Hillside Rd *FAL* TR11 .... 53 H3
Holly Cl *RTRUS* TR3 .... 14 D3
Holywell Rd *RTRUS* TR3 .... 24 C5
Hugus Rd *RTRUS* TR3 .... 15 E3
Hull's La *FAL* TR11 .... 4 E4
Hunkin Cl *TRU* TR1 .... 3 F2
Hurland Rd *TRU* TR1 .... 3 G7
Huthnance Cl *TRU* TR1 .... 17 H2 ▣

I

Idless La *RTRUNW* TR4........................ 8 B2
Infirmary Hl *TRU* TR1 .... 3 F6

J

Jacks Cl *PENRYN* TR10 .... 47 F4 ▣
James Pl *TRU* TR1 .... 3 H4
Jennings Rd *PENRYN* TR10................ 46 B5
John St *TRU* TR1................................. 2 E4
Jubilee Rd *FAL* TR11 .... 4 A1
   RTRUS TR3 .... 14 D3

K

Keeble Pk *RTRUS* TR3...................... 31 E3
Kelley Rd *FAL* TR11 .... 53 G1
Kelliwith *RTRUS* TR3 .... 32 D3
Kemp Cl *TRU* TR1 .... 3 H4
Kenna Rd *TRU* TR1 .... 16 B3 ▣
Kenwyn Church Rd *TRU* TR1.............. 2 D1
Kenwyn Hl *RTRUNW* TR4 .... 16 D1
Kenwyn Rd *RTRUNW* TR4 .... 8 C5
   TRU TR1 .... 2 D2
Kenwyn St *TRU* TR1 .... 3 F4
Kergilliack Rd *FAL* TR11 .... 53 E1
Kerley Gv *TRU* TR1 .... 16 B3
Kernick Rd *PENRYN* TR10................. 46 C4
Kerris Gv *TRU* TR1 .... 2 C2
Kersey Rd *FAL* TR11 .... 48 B5
Kestle Dr *TRU* TR1 .... 16 B3
Killigrew St *FAL* TR11 .... 4 C3
Kimberley Pl *FAL* TR11 .... 4 B3 ▣
King's Av *FAL* TR11............................ 53 H2
Kingsley Cl *RTRUS* TR3 .... 15 G3
Kings Rd *RTRUE/STMW* TR2 .... 56 B1
King St *TRU* TR1 .... 3 G4
Kirby Rd *TRU* TR1.............................. 2 A4
Knights Hl *TRU* TR1.......................... 16 D1
Knight's Mdw *RTRUS* TR3................. 31 H2
Knoll Pk *TRU* TR1 .... 17 H3

L

Laburnum Cl *FAL* TR11 .... 47 H5
Laburnum Dr *FAL* TR11 .... 53 H1 ▣
Ladock Rd *RTRUE/STMW* TR2 .... 12 D1
Lambs La *FAL* TR11 .... 53 G1
Lamellyn Dr *TRU* TR1 .... 15 H3
Lanaton Rd *PENRYN* TR10................. 46 C4
Langarth Cl *RTRUS* TR3..................... 15 E2
Langton Rd *FAL* TR11 .... 48 A5
Lanoweth *PENRYN* TR10 .... 46 D2
Lansdowne Rd *FAL* TR11 .... 4 E5
Lanyon Rd *RTRUS* TR3 .... 24 C5
La Vague *RTRUS* TR3 .... 41 E1
Leap Pk *RTRUS* TR3 .... 14 D3
The Leas *TRU* TR1 .... 3 K2 ▣
The Leats *TRU* TR1 .... 3 F4
Lemon Hl *FAL* TR11 .... 40 A5
Lemon Mews Rd *TRU* TR1 .... 3 F5
Lemon Quay *TRU* TR1 .... 3 G5
Lemon St *TRU* TR1............................. 3 F6
Lewman Cl *RTRUE/STMW* TR2 .... 12 C2
Lewman Rd *RTRUE/STMW* TR2 .... 12 C2 ▣
Lighterage Hl *TRU* TR1..................... 25 F1
Link Cl *FAL* TR11 .... 53 H3
Linley Cl *RTRUS* TR3 .... 15 E3 ▣
Lister Hl *FAL* TR11 .... 4 B3
Lister St *FAL* TR11 .... 4 B3
Little Castle St *TRU* TR1 .... 3 F4 ▣
Little Oaks *PENRYN* TR10.................. 46 D4
Lodge Dr *TRU* TR1............................. 17 H1
Longfield *FAL* TR11 .... 53 G2
Love La *PENRYN* TR10........................ 47 F3
Lowen Wy *RTRUS* TR3 .... 14 D3
Lower Castle Rd
   RTRUE/STMW TR2 .... 56 A2
Lower Hugus Rd *RTRUS* TR3 .... 14 D4
Lower Pk *RTRUE/STMW* TR2 .... 11 F4
Lower Polstain Rd *RTRUS* TR3 .... 15 E4
Lower Redannick *TRU* TR1 .... 2 E5
Lower St *PENRYN* TR10...................... 47 E3
The Lugger *RTRUE/STMW* TR2 .... 51 H2
Lukes Cl *TRU* TR1 .... 17 H2
Lychgate Dr *TRU* TR1 .... 2 D1

M

Madeira Wk *FAL* TR11 .... 4 B7
Malabar Rd *FAL* TR11 .... 16 A3
Malpas Rd *TRU* TR1 .... 3 H5
Manor Cl *FAL* TR11............................ 53 G1
Manor Crs *FAL* TR11.......................... 53 G1

Manor Rd *FAL* TR11 .... 53 G1
Manse Rd *RTRUS* TR3 .... 31 H2
Marine Pde *RTRUE/STMW* TR2 .... 56 A2
Market Strd *FAL* TR11 .... 4 C1
Market St *FAL* TR11........................... 4 C2
   RTRUS TR3 .... 31 G4
Marlborough Av *FAL* TR11 .... 4 A5
Marlborough Crs *FAL* TR11 .... 4 A4
Marlborough Gv *FAL* TR11................. 4 A5
Marlborough Rd *FAL* TR11 .... 4 C4
Mayfield Rd *FAL* TR11 .... 53 H2
Meadowbank *FAL* TR11 .... 40 B5 ▣
Meadowbank Rd *FAL* TR11 .... 48 A5
Meadow Cl *RTRUS* TR3 .... 15 G3 ▣
Meadow La *TRU* TR1 .... 3 G7
Meadowside Rd *FAL* TR11 .... 53 H3
Mearwood La *FAL* TR11 .... 53 H2 ▣
Melvill Crs *FAL* TR11 .... 4 D5
Melville Rd *RTRUS* TR3 .... 14 D3 ▣
Melvill La *FAL* TR11 .... 4 D6
Melvill Rd *FAL* TR11 .... 4 C5
Merrick Av *TRU* TR1 .... 3 K1
Merrifield Cl *TRU* TR1 .... 2 D3
Merrill Pl *FAL* TR11............................ 4 B4
Messack Cl *FAL* TR11 .... 53 G4
Midway Dr *TRU* TR1 .... 3 K1
Military Rd *RTRUE/STMW* TR2 .... 56 C4
Mill Hl *RTRUE/STMW* TR2 .... 42 D5
Mill La *TRU* TR1................................. 24 D1
Minnie Pl *FAL* TR11 .... 4 D4
Mitchell Hl *TRU* TR1 .... 3 H3
Mongleath Av *FAL* TR11 .... 53 G3
Mongleath Cl *FAL* TR11 .... 53 G4
Mongleath Rd *FAL* TR11 .... 53 G3
Monterey Gdns *TRU* TR1 .... 3 J2
Moresk Cl *TRU* TR1 .... 3 G2
Moresk Rd *TRU* TR1 .... 3 G2
Morlaix Av *TRU* TR1 .... 3 H5
Mount Agar Rd *RTRUS* TR3 .... 31 H2 ▣
Mount Pleasant Rd *RTRUS* TR3... 15 F3
Mount Stephens La *FAL* TR11 ..... 53 H2 ▣
Murdoch Cl *TRU* TR1 .... 3 J1

N

Nancemere Rd *TRU* TR1 .... 3 H1
Nangitha Cl *FAL* TR11 .... 53 E3 ▣
Nansavallon Rd *RTRUS* TR3 .... 15 H3 ▣
Newbridge La *RTRUS* TR3 .... 15 H4
New Bridge St *TRU* TR1 .... 3 H4
Newbridge Wy *TRU* TR1 .... 15 H3
Newham Rd *TRU* TR1 .... 3 H7 ▣
   TRU TR1 .... 25 G1
New Mills La *RTRUNW* TR4 .... 16 B1
Newquay Rd *TRU* TR1 .... 9 G5
New Rw *FAL* TR11 .... 40 A5
New St *FAL* TR11 .... 4 D3
   PENRYN TR10 .... 47 F4
Newton Pk *RTRUE/STMW* TR2 .... 56 A1
Newton Rd *RTRUE/STMW* TR2 .... 50 B5
New Windsor Ter *FAL* TR11 .... 4 B4
Norfolk Rd *FAL* TR11 .... 4 C3
Northey Cl *RTRUNW* TR4 .... 8 B2
Northfield Dr *TRU* TR1 .... 3 F7
North Pde *FAL* TR11 .... 48 A5
   RTRUS TR3 .... 51 H2
The Nurseries *FAL* TR11 .... 53 F1
Nursery Cl *TRU* TR1 .... 3 G2 ▣

O

Oakfield Rd *FAL* TR11 .... 53 H1
Oakland Pk *FAL* TR11......................... 53 E1
Oak Wy *TRU* TR1 .... 3 F3
Old Bridge St *TRU* TR1 .... 3 G4
Old Carnon Hl *RTRUS* TR3................ 31 G4
Old Coach Rd *RTRUS* TR3................. 24 C4
Old Falmouth Rd *TRU* TR1 .... 25 E1
Old Hl *FAL* TR11 .... 54 A1
Old Hill Crs *FAL* TR11 .... 53 H1
Old Tram Rd *RTRUS* TR3 .... 32 A4
Old Well Gdns *PENRYN* TR10 ...... 47 E2 ▣
Olivey Pl *FAL* TR11 .... 40 A4 ▣
Orchard Cl *TRU* TR1 .... 16 B3
Owan Hts *TRU* TR1 .... 16 B4

P

Packsaddle *PENRYN* TR10................. 46 C2
Packsaddle Cl *PENRYN* TR10 .... 46 C2
Parc-an-challow
   PENRYN TR10 .... 46 D3 ▣

Parc-an-dillon Rd
   RTRUE/STMW TR2 ....
Parc-an-gwarry *RTRUS* TR3 .... 3▯
Parc Briwer *PENRYN* TR10 4
Parc Merys *RTRUE/STMW* TR2 .. 51
Parc Peneglos *FAL* TR11................ 40
Parkancreeg *RTRUS* TR3 31
Park Crs *FAL* TR11 ....
Parkengear Vean
   RTRUE/STMW TR2 ....
Park Hl *FAL* TR11 ....
Park La *FAL* TR11 ....
Park Ri *FAL* TR11 ....
Park Ter *FAL* TR11 ....
Park Vw *FAL* TR11 ....
Park View Cl *RTRUS* TR3.................
Passage Hl *FAL* TR11 ....
Paul's Ter *TRU* TR1 ....
Pedn-Moran *RTRUE/STMW* TR2 .....
Pellew Rd *FAL* TR11 ....
Penair Crs *TRU* TR1 ....
Penair Vw *TRU* TR1 ....
Penarrow Cl *FAL* TR11 53
Penarrow Rd *FAL* TR11.....................
Penarth Rd *FAL* TR11 ....
Pen Brea Cl *RTRUE/STMW* TR2 ... 50
Pencantol *RTRUS* TR3 ....
Pendale Sq *TRU* TR1 ....
Pendarves Rd *FAL* TR11 ....
   TRU TR1 ....
Pendeen Cl *RTRUS* TR3....................
Pendeen Crs *RTRUS* TR3 ....
Pendeen Rd *RTRUS* TR3 ....
   TRU TR1 ....
Pendennis Rd *FAL* TR11 ....
Pendower Rd *RTRUE/STMW* TR2 ... 3
Pengarth Cl *TRU* TR1 17
Pengarth Ri *FAL* TR11 ....
Pengarth Rd *FAL* TR11 ....
Pengelly Wy *RTRUS* TR3 ....
Penhale Rd *FAL* TR11 5
Penhaligon Ct *TRU* TR1 ....
Penhallow Cl *RTRUE/STMW* TR2 .. 3
Penhalls Wy *RTRUS* TR3 ....
Penmere Crs *FAL* TR11 ....
Penmere Hl *FAL* TR11 ....
Penmere Pl *FAL* TR11 ....
Penmorvah *FAL* TR11 48
Penmorvah Rd *TRU* TR1 ....
Pennance Rd *FAL* TR11 ....
Penoweth *FAL* TR11 48
Penpol Hl *RTRUS* TR3 3
Penrose Rd *FAL* TR11 ....
Penruan La *RTRUE/STMW* TR2 5
Pensilva Rd *TRU* TR1 1
Pentire Rd *PENRYN* TR10................. 4
Penvale Crs *PENRYN* TR10 4
Penvale Dr *PENRYN* TR10................. 4
Penvean Cl *PENRYN* TR10 46
Penvean La *TRU* TR1 5
Penventinnie La *RTRUNW* TR4 ....
Penwarne Rd *FAL* TR11 5
Penwerris La *FAL* TR11 1
Penwerris Rd *FAL* TR11....................
Penwethers La *TRU* TR1...................
Percuil Vw *RTRUE/STMW* TR2 5
Permarin Rd *PENRYN* TR10 4
Perran Cl *RTRUS* TR3 31
Pike's Hl *FAL* TR11 ....
Pillars Rd *FAL* TR11...........................
Pit Meadow *FAL* TR11 53
Place View Rd
   RTRUE/STMW TR2 56
Point Rd *RTRUS* TR3 .... 3▯
Polmennor Rd *FAL* TR11................. 5▯
Polsethow *PENRYN* TR10.............. 4▯
Polstain Crs *RTRUS* TR3 15
Polstain Rd *RTRUS* TR3 .... 1▯
Polsue Wy *RTRUE/STMW* TR2 ...... 1▯
Poltair Rd *PENRYN* TR10..................
Poltisko Rd *PENRYN* TR10 .... 4▯
Poltisko Ter *PENRYN* TR10.............. 4▯
Polvarth Rd *RTRUE/STMW* TR2 .. 56
Polventon Cl *FAL* TR11 53
Polwhele Rd *TRU* TR1 17
Polwithen Rd *FAL* TR11 4
   PENRYN TR10 46
Porth Vw *RTRUE/STMW* TR2 .... 5▯
Portland Gdns *FAL* TR11................. 53
Pound La *RTRUS* TR3......................... 23
Praze Meadow *PENRYN* TR10 47
The Praze *PENRYN* TR10.................. 47
Prince's St *TRU* TR1 ....
Prislow Cl *FAL* TR11 53
Prislow Flds *FAL* TR11 ....
Prislow La *FAL* TR11......................... 53
Pydar St *TRU* TR1..............................

Q

y HI *FAL* TR11	4 C2
HI *FAL* TR11	4 D3
RYN TR10	47 F4
Rd *FAL* TR11	40 C2
US TR3	31 G5
St *FAL* TR11	4 E3
TR1	3 H4
uay *RTRUE/STMW* TR2	56 B1
Anne Gdns *FAL* TR11	53 G3
Mary Ct *FAL* TR11	4 C7
Mary Rd *FAL* TR11	4 D7
chwell Rd *RTRUS* TR3	23 H5

R

HI *RTRUNW* TR4	22 A5
gh Pl *FAL* TR11	4 B3
eigh V *TRU* TR1	3 K4 🔲
nnick Crs *TRU* TR1	2 D6
nnick La *TRU* TR1	2 D5
onguet HI *FAL* TR11	40 C3
rds Crs *TRU* TR1	16 B3
nond HI *TRU* TR1	2 D4
nond Pl *TRU* TR1	2 D4 🔲
nond Ter *TRU* TR1	2 D4 🔲
eway *RTRUE/STMW* TR2	12 D2
side Vw *TRU* TR1	3 J7
St *RTRUE/STMW* TR2	51 H2
J TR1	3 F4
a La *RTRUE/STMW* TR2	56 A1
rt Hichens Rd *FAL* TR11	54 A1
y La *RTRUE/STMW* TR2	44 C1
walk HI *TRU* TR1	25 E1
arrack Ct *FAL* TR11	53 G4
arrack Rd *FAL* TR11	53 E5
dale Rd *FAL* TR11	2 E2
Eglos Cl *FAL* TR11	53 E4 🔲
nill *FAL* TR11	48 A1
land Gdns	
RUE/STMW TR2	37 G4
valley *RTRUS* TR3	15 E3 🔲
arc *RTRUE/STMW* TR2	13 E2
d Ring *PENRYN* TR10	47 F3

S

nthony Wy *FAL* TR11	4 B7
bryn's Rd *TRU* TR1	3 G6
ustell Rw	
RUE/STMW TR2	56 B1 🔲
ement's Cl *TRU* TR1	3 K4
ement's HI *TRU* TR1	3 J4
ements Parc *TRU* TR1	3 K5 🔲
ement St *TRU* TR1	3 G3
ominic Sq *TRU* TR1	2 E4 🔲
ominic St *TRU* TR1	2 E4
eorge's Rd *TRU* TR1	3 F1
uvias Parc *PENRYN* TR10	47 F3 🔲
uvias St *PENRYN* TR10	47 F4
eyne Ter *RTRUS* TR3	31 G4
ary's St *TRU* TR1	3 G4
cholas St *TRU* TR1	3 G4
eter's Rd *FAL* TR11	3 H4 🔲
ran's HI *RTRUS* TR3	30 D5
nomas Cl *RTRUS* TR3	16 B3 🔲
nomas St *PENRYN* TR10	47 F4
sbury Rd *TRU* TR1	2 D5 🔲
box Cl *FAL* TR11	48 A1
box Rd *FAL* TR11	48 A1
pson Wy *RTRUS* TR3	15 E3 🔲

Saracen Crs *PENRYN* TR10	47 E4
Saracen Pl *PENRYN* TR10	47 E4 🔲
Saracen Wy *PENRYN* TR10	47 E4
School HI *RTRUNW* TR4	8 B2
RTRUS TR3	30 C5
School La *FAL* TR11	53 E3
TRU TR1	2 E7
Sea View Crs *RTRUE/STMW* TR2	56 B1
Sea View Rd *FAL* TR11	53 H2
Seymour Cl *RTRUS* TR3	14 D3 🔲
Shelburne Rd *FAL* TR11	53 H2
Shute La *PENRYN* TR10	47 E3 🔲
Shute Meadow *PENRYN* TR10	47 E4 🔲
Silver HI *RTRUS* TR3	30 D3
Silver Wy *RTRUS* TR3	14 D3 🔲
Slades La *PENRYN* TR10	47 E4 🔲
Smithick HI *FAL* TR11	4 D2
Smithy La *RTRUS* TR3	31 H2
South Vw *PENRYN* TR10	47 E3
South West Coast Pth *FAL* TR11	4 A7
RTRUE/STMW TR2	45 H3
Spargo Ct *PENRYN* TR10	46 A5 🔲
Speech La *RTRUS* TR3	38 A3
Spernen Wyn Rd *FAL* TR11	4 B6
The Spires *FAL* TR11	2 E1
Springfield Pk *FAL* TR11	40 A4
Springfield Rd *FAL* TR11	53 G2 🔲
Springfield Wy *RTRUS* TR3	14 D3
The Square *RTRUE/STMW* TR2	37 H4
RTRUE/STMW TR2	51 H2
Staggy La *RTRUS* TR3	31 H2
Station Rd *PENRYN* TR10	46 D3
RTRUS TR3	30 D3
TRU TR1	2 B4
Stephney Pk *FAL* TR11	53 E4
Stokes Rd *FAL* TR11	2 E3
Stracey Rd *FAL* TR11	4 D6
Strangways Ter *TRU* TR1	3 F6
Stretyn *RTRUS* TR3	31 H1
Summerheath *PENRYN* TR10	46 B4
Sunningdale *TRU* TR1	2 B4
Swanpool HI *FAL* TR11	4 A6
Swanpool Rd *FAL* TR11	54 A5
Swanpool St *FAL* TR11	4 D2
Swanvale Rd *FAL* TR11	53 H3 🔲
Symons HI *FAL* TR11	54 A1

T

Tabernacle St *TRU* TR1	3 G5
Tarrandean La *RTRUS* TR3	31 E3
Theydon Rd *TRU* TR1	3 G5
Tollyfrank HI *RTRUE/STMW* TR2	37 G4
Trebartha Rd *TRU* TR1	17 H2
Tredenham Rd	
RTRUE/STMW TR2	56 C1
Tredova Crs *FAL* TR11	4 C7
Tredrea Gdns *RTRUS* TR3	30 D5
Tredynas Rd *FAL* TR11	5 H5
Tredyson Pl *FAL* TR11	4 A4
Tre-el-Verne Cl *TRU* TR1	2 A5 🔲
Trefusis Cl *TRU* TR1	17 H2
Trefusis Rd *FAL* TR11	48 B5
FAL TR11	53 G4
Tregassick Rd *RTRUE/STMW* TR2	51 F3
Tregavethan Vw *RTRUS* TR3	14 D2
Tregear Gdns *TRU* TR1	3 F4
Tregenver Rd *FAL* TR11	53 H3
Tregenver Vls *FAL* TR11	53 H3
Tregew Cl *FAL* TR11	48 B4
Tregew Rd *FAL* TR11	48 A3
Tregolls Cl *TRU* TR1	3 J3
Tregolls Rd *TRU* TR1	3 J3
Tregony Rd *RTRUE/STMW* TR2	12 D2
Tregothnan Rd *RTRUS* TR3	53 H1
TRU TR1	17 G5 🔲
Tregullow Rd *FAL* TR11	53 G1
Tregunter Ms *FAL* TR11	5 G4 🔲

Tregurra La *TRU* TR1	17 G1
Tregye Rd *RTRUS* TR3	32 A2
Trehaverne La *TRU* TR1	2 E2
Trekeen Rd *PENRYN* TR10	46 D3 🔲
Trelander Barton *TRU* TR1	3 K3 🔲
Trelander East *TRU* TR1	17 H3
Trelander Hwy *TRU* TR1	3 K4
Trelander North *TRU* TR1	3 K4
Trelander South *TRU* TR1	17 H3
Trelawne Cl *RTRUS* TR3	31 H2 🔲
Trelawne Rd *RTRUS* TR3	31 G2
Trelawney Av *FAL* TR11	4 D5
Trelawney Rd *RTRUE/STMW* TR2	56 A1
TRU TR1	2 D2
Trelawny Rd *FAL* TR11	4 C3
Treleaver Wy *TRU* TR1	16 B4
Treliever Rd *PENRYN* TR10	46 B4
Trelil La *FAL* TR11	53 E4
Treliske La *TRU* TR1	16 B2
Trelissick Rd *FAL* TR11	53 H1
Treloan La *RTRUE/STMW* TR2	51 G2
Tremanor Wy *FAL* TR11	53 F1 🔲
Tremarne Cl *RTRUS* TR3	41 E1
Tremayne Cl *RTRUS* TR3	31 G4
Tremayne Rd *TRU* TR1	2 E3
Tremorvah Barton *TRU* TR1	3 K3 🔲
Tremorvah Crs *TRU* TR1	3 J2
Tremorvah Wood La *TRU* TR1	3 J2
Trenarth *PENRYN* TR10	47 E4 🔲
Treneglos *RTRUS* TR3	30 A2
Trenerry Cl *TRU* TR1	3 H1
Trennick La *TRU* TR1	3 J5
Tresahar Rd *FAL* TR11	53 G4
Tresawle Rd *FAL* TR11	48 A5
Tresawls Av *TRU* TR1	15 H3
Tresawls Rd *RTRUNW* TR4	14 C2
RTRUS TR3	15 G2
TRU TR1	15 H3
Trescobeas Rd *FAL* TR11	53 F1
Tresco Pl *FAL* TR11	53 H2
Treseder's Gdns *TRU* TR1	3 G2
Tresillian Rd *FAL* TR11	47 H5
Tresooth La *PENRYN* TR10	46 D3
Tresowgar La *RTRUE/STMW* TR2	12 B2
Trevance *PENRYN* TR10	46 C4
Trevanion Ct *TRU* TR1	16 B3
Trevarth Rd *FAL* TR11	53 G1
Trevaylor Cl *TRU* TR1	3 J1
Trevaylor Rd *FAL* TR11	53 H1
Trevean Rd *TRU* TR1	16 A3
Treveglos Rd *FAL* TR11	53 G5
Trevellan Rd *FAL* TR11	40 A5
Trevelva Rd *TRU* TR1	17 G5
Treventon Cl *FAL* TR11	53 G2 🔲
RTRUE/STMW TR2	51 G2 🔲
Treventon Rd *RTRUE/STMW* TR2	51 G2
Treverbyn Ri *PENRYN* TR10	46 C3
Treverbyn Rd *TRU* TR1	17 G1
Treveryn Pk *FAL* TR11	53 E4
Trevethan Cl *FAL* TR11	4 A2
Trevethan Gdns *FAL* TR11	4 B2 🔲
Trevethan HI *FAL* TR11	4 C1 🔲
Trevethan Ri *FAL* TR11	4 A2
Trevethan Rd *FAL* TR11	4 B2
Trevethenick Rd *TRU* TR1	3 J6
Treviglas La *RTRUE/STMW* TR2	12 C2
Treviglas Ri *RTRUE/STMW* TR2	12 C2
Trevithick Cl *TRU* TR1	3 J2
Trevithick Rd *RTRUS* TR3	53 G1
TRU TR1	3 K1
Trevoney *FAL* TR11	53 E3
Trevose Rd *TRU* TR1	16 A2
Trewarton Rd *PENRYN* TR10	46 D2
Trewen Rd *FAL* TR11	53 E5
Trewidden Cl *TRU* TR1	3 K3
Trewinnard Rd *RTRUS* TR3	30 C5
Treworder Rd *TRU* TR1	2 D6
Treworthal Rd *RTRUS* TR3	30 C5
Treyew Rd *TRU* TR1	2 B5
Trolver HI *RTRUS* TR3	32 D4

Truck HI *RTRUE/STMW* TR2	12 B2
Truro HI *PENRYN* TR10	47 E3
Truro La *PENRYN* TR10	47 E3
Truro Vean Ter *TRU* TR1	3 G3
Turnaware Rd *FAL* TR11	53 G4

U

Union Cnr *FAL* TR11	53 F1
Union HI *TRU* TR1	18 A1
Union Pl *TRU* TR1	3 G4
Union Rd *FAL* TR11	47 F5
Union St *TRU* TR1	3 F4
Upland Cl *TRU* TR1	17 H2
Upland Crs *TRU* TR1	3 K1
Upper Castle Rd	
RTRUE/STMW TR2	56 A1
Upper Tredrea *RTRUS* TR3	30 D5

V

Valley Cl *TRU* TR1	16 A3
Valley La *RTRUS* TR3	31 H1
Valley View Dr *TRU* TR1	16 A3
Venton Rd *FAL* TR11	53 G2
Vernon Pl *FAL* TR11	4 C2
Vicarage Cl *FAL* TR11	53 E3
Vicarage HI *FAL* TR11	53 E3
Victoria Gdns *RTRUS* TR3	15 E3
Victoria Rd *RTRUS* TR3	15 E3
Victoria Sq *TRU* TR1	3 F4

W

Wagg La *RTRUE/STMW* TR2	12 D3
Waterings Rd *FAL* TR11	40 A5
Waterloo *TRU* TR1	3 J4
Waterloo Cl *RTRUE/STMW* TR2	50 B5
Waterloo Rd *FAL* TR11	4 C3
Water Smead Parc *FAL* TR11	53 E3
Water Smead Pk *FAL* TR11	53 E3
Wayfield Rd *FAL* TR11	48 D2
Webber St *FAL* TR11	4 C2
Wellington Plantation	
RTRUS TR3	32 D2
Wellington Ter *FAL* TR11	4 C3
West Cnr *RTRUS* TR3	31 H1 🔲
West End Cl *PENRYN* TR10	47 E3
Western Pl *PENRYN* TR10	46 D3 🔲
Western Ter *FAL* TR11	4 B4
Westmoor Crs *RTRUS* TR3	30 C4
West Pk *RTRUS* TR3	30 C4
West Pl *FAL* TR11	4 B4
West Ri *FAL* TR11	53 H3
West St *PENRYN* TR10	47 E3
Whitley Cl *TRU* TR1	3 H4 🔲
Wilkes Wk *TRU* TR1	3 G4
William St *TRU* TR1	3 G6
Willow Cl *FAL* TR11	40 A5
Windmill HI *RTRUE/STMW* TR2	50 B2
Windsor Ct *FAL* TR11	4 B4
Windsor Ter *FAL* TR11	4 B3
Wodehouse Ter *FAL* TR11	4 C2
Woodland Av *PENRYN* TR10	46 D4
Woodland Ri *PENRYN* TR10	46 D4
Woodlane *FAL* TR11	4 B6
Woodlane Crs *FAL* TR11	4 C4
Woodlane Dr *FAL* TR11	4 D4
Woodside *PENRYN* TR10	46 D4 🔲
Wood Vw *PENRYN* TR10	46 D5
Woodway *PENRYN* TR10	46 D5 🔲
Woon La *RTRUS* TR3	31 H1 🔲

Index - featured places

nbishop Benson School	
TRU TR1	3 H2
con County Junior School	
FAL TR11	4 A1
con Infant School	
FAL TR11	4 A1
keley Gallery	
FAL TR11	4 C1
u Gallery	
PENRYN TR10	47 F4

Bosvigo County Primary School	
TRU TR1	2 D5
Budock Hospital	
FAL TR11	53 F1
Carrick Business Centre	
PENRYN TR10	47 F4
Carrick Sports Centre	
TRU TR1	2 D3
Cathedral	
TRU TR1	3 G4

City Hospital	
TRU TR1	2 E5
College of Further	
& Higher Education	
FAL TR11	4 C3
Cornwall Maritime Museum	
FAL TR11	4 D2
Court Gallery	
TRU TR1	3 F4
Cusgarne School	
RTRUS TR3	30 A1

The Duchy Hospital	
RTRUNW TR4	15 H1
Eastwood Park Estate	
PENRYN TR10	47 F4
Falmouth Business Park	
FAL TR11	53 G3
Falmouth College of Arts	
FAL TR11	4 C5
Falmouth Community School	
FAL TR11	53 G1

Falmouth & District Hospital
FAL TR11 .... **53** H2

Falmouth Golf Club
FAL TR11 .... **53** H5

Falmouth Lower School
FAL TR11 .... **53** H2

Falmouth Tennis Club
FAL TR11 .... **4** B5

Flushing Sailing Club
PENRYN TR10 .... **48** B5

The Gallery
TRU TR1 .... **3** H4

Gerrans Primary School
RTRUE/STMW TR2 .... **51** G3

Glass House Gallery
TRU TR1 .... **3** F5

Kea Junior & Infant School
RTRUS TR3 .... **24** D2

Kernick Business Park
PENRYN TR10 .... **46** C5

King Charles VC Junior
& Infant School
FAL TR11 .... **4** C5

Lower Newham Industrial Estate
TRU TR1 .... **3** H7

Mabe County Primary School
PENRYN TR10 .... **46** B4

Malins Hall Gallery
FAL TR11 .... **4** C1

Morning Price Gallery
FAL TR11 .... **4** D2

Morrab Studio & Art Gallery
TRU TR1 .... **3** G5

National Maritime
Museum Cornwall
FAL TR11 .... **4** B3

The Old Barn Gallery
RTRUS TR3 .... **30** D5

Penair School
TRU TR1 .... **18** A2

Pencalenick School
TRU TR1 .... **18** D2

Pendennis Castle
FAL TR11 .... **5** K6

Penryn Community School
PENRYN TR10 .... **46** C4

Penryn Junior & Infant School
PENRYN TR10 .... **46** D3

Penryn Rugby Club
PENRYN TR10 .... **46** C4

The Penryn Surgery
PENRYN TR10 .... **47** E4

Polwele House School
RTRUNW TR4 .... **9** H3

Probus CP School
RTRUE/STMW TR2 .... **12** D1

Redannick Theatre
TRU TR1 .... **2** E5

Richard Lander School
TRU TR1 .... **16** A3

Royal Cornwall Hospital
RTRUNW TR4 .... **15** H2

Royal Cornwall Museum
TRU TR1 .... **2** E4

Royal Cornwall Yacht Club
FAL TR11 .... **54** B1

St Francis C of E School
FAL TR11 .... **53** F3

St Marys Junior & Infant School
TRU TR1 .... **2** E1

St Marys School
FAL TR11 .... **53** G3

St Mawes CP School
RTRUE/STMW TR2 .... **56** B1

St Mawes Sailing Club
RTRUE/STMW TR2 .... **56** B1

St Michaels Catholic
Small School
TRU TR1 .... **2** E4

Shortlanesend School
RTRUNW TR4 .... **8** B2

Threemilestone County Primary
School
RTRUS TR3 .... **15** E3

Threemilestone Surgery
RTRUS TR3 .... **15** E3

Tregolls CP School
TRU TR1 .... **17** H2

Treliske Hospital
RTRUNW TR4 .... **15** H2

Trewithen
RTRUE/STMW TR2 .... **13** H2

Treyew CP School
TRU TR1 .... **2** A4

Truro Bowl
TRU TR1 ....

Truro City AFC
TRU TR1 ....

Truro College
RTRUS TR3 ....

Truro College
RTRUS TR3 ....

Truro College
TRU TR1 ....

Truro Golf Club
TRU TR1 ....

Truro High School for Girls
TRU TR1 ....

Truro Rugby Football Club
TRU TR1 ....

Truro School
TRU TR1 ....

Veryan Junior & Infant School
RTRUE/STMW TR2 ....

West End Industrial Estate
PENRYN TR10 ....

Westover Surgery
FAL TR11 ....

Woodlane Surgery
FAL TR11 ....

Wren Industrial Estate
RTRUS TR3 ....

YHA
FAL TR11 ....

Notes